|GENERATION

Tom Stolz

WWW.GENERATION-BOOK.COM

|GENERATION

Generation Publishing, Portage, Michigan 49024

WWW.GENERATION-BOOK.COM

© 2012 Tom Stolz

Cover Design: Jonah Stolz
Edited By: Jonah Stolz, Samantha Stolz

ISBN-13: 978-0615633978 (Generation Publishing)
ISBN-10: 0615633978

Dedication and Thanks

This book is dedicated to my sons Noah, Jonah, and Luke. Nothing compares to the opportunity to watch you grow into the men God designed you to be. You have given me so much to be proud of already, and getting to be your dad is much more than I deserve. The prayer constantly in my heart and on my lips is that you would be men after His own heart.

Thanks to my wife, Samantha, for causing me to believe that I can do anything, and helping me be confident that I hear Him. The support you have shown me since the day we met, even when I have least deserved it, has made ALL the difference in my life. I cannot imagine life apart from you. You are my everything on earth. You get all my love.

Thanks to Barb Fay and Carol Dunning for telling me to write a book. It prepared my heart to receive God's assignment. Thanks also to my Mom (Sharon Stolz) and my family, as well as my extended family at Agape Christian Church. I can't tell you how much I appreciate your comments of encouragement, support, and your prayers.

Thanks to my Grandma, Joyce Sweet. You demonstrated wholeheartedness to me before I had ever heard the term. Your legacy of prayer for our family humbles me and convicts me. The earth has been permanently marked by your life. I love you and Grandpa more than words can express.

Table of Contents

Introduction - 1 1

Love: The Ultimate Battle Plan - 2 7

The Ancient Highway - 3 27

Jesus Wants to What?! - 4 59

Think About Heaven! - 5 77

Authority: Resist and Enemy Will Flee! - 6 97

Rise of the End-Time Worship Movements - 7.............122

Where Do We Go From Here? - 8 145

Introduction - 1

This book is a message to my sons, but the Lord told me to send it to a generation. When I consider how quickly the world is changing, it creates a whirlwind of emotion in my heart. I remember the way things used to be, and am tempted to long for what seems like lost innocence. I remember playing in the woods and knowing nothing of child abductors, or human trafficking, or the awful affairs of leaders and sports heroes. I remember being able to roam my small town all day, only needing to be back for dinner. But this is really an idealized memory. The truth is, the world has been changing for a long time. As soon as Adam and Eve took the first bite of fruit from the Tree of the Knowledge of Good and Evil, as the juice was still on their chin, decay entered the world.

The Bible says that as all creation groans with the weight of the fall, and God's amazing and terrifying plan for the culmination of the renewal of creation is near, that knowledge will increase and people will rush from place to place. It's official, knowledge has certainly increased. My sons know it, almost too well. From the time they were born they could order a pizza from a computer, find out who the leader of Pakistan was, or find out where the last 50 earthquakes took place as easily as they could find out the current time. With the push of a button, centuries of knowledge are at our fingertips.

My boys have traveled more in the ten short years of their lives together than the last three generations of my family did, combined. But this increase in knowledge has come with a price: an acute awareness of the state of creation. The internet and media have given us an inside look into the real heart of man, with all its beauty and tragedy. The slow movement of knowledge acted as a buffer until this last generation. Somehow the distance of news stories gave us comfort, and the economy of words and print space kept the fringe elements of society from our eyes and ears.

With the incredible increase of information, that buffer is lost. Comfort is an antique when it comes to the knowledge of the state of our culture. The fringe element is the news. The more absurd, or devastating, or shocking the news story, the more quickly it propagates in a media where economy no longer matters. Volume and pace are the measurements that define media success. We live in a time when the news is the one thing we don't want our kids in the room to hear. But they hear it...

...you guys hear it, don't you? You hear it, and you try to make sense of it, and you see all the people around you acting like it is kind of normal, and everything will be ok...but you know that is not quite right. You know something different is happening, but you are not quite sure what it all means.

I am writing this message to **you** to help you understand what it means. My prayer, and the fire burning in my heart for this message, is that it will help you see what an exciting and blessed time you live in. When I was a young guy and I received a book about the Bible, or a book about God, I welcomed it on my shelf, right next to my Bible. When my mom made me clean my room, I would dust it off right along with my Bible and then put it all right back in the same spot. We want to treat the Bible as special, but boring; kind of like the football or soccer trophy you won when you were eight. I am praying this book changes your mind about the Bible. I pray that it will turn your Bible from a trophy into a treasure map (if you are a guy), or a romance novel of epic proportions (if you are a lady). That is truly what the Bible is, a treasure map and an epic story. God's Word tells a story that you are living out in real-time.

The world is just getting to the X-that-marks-the-spot or the scene where the hero is about to rush in to save the day. You live in a time all of creation has longed to see unfold, and you have a front row seat. How the next years look to you will really depend on the lens you look through. Think 3-D glasses: if you have the glasses on, everything in the movie looks right and is exciting. Without the glasses, you get a headache and want to go home. I would like to help you put on the glasses!

I have lived for nearly 40 years, most of those knowing at least a little about Jesus. I have to tell you, I am more excited about Jesus and what He is doing right now than I have ever been. The more I find out about His plans for me, and the time of history that I am living in, the more fascinated I am with who He is. Yes....FASCINATED.

I have not always felt this way about Jesus. This relationship with God is really new for me. I used to think of him as powerful, really nice, kind of close, but still unimaginably far away. I guessed He loved me like He loves everyone else. Him on His throne, me in a sea of people. These ideas seemed right, but they never really moved my heart. They never made me want to completely sell out to Him. I used to want a comfortable amount of Jesus. Enough to save me from Hell, make me feel good about Sunday morning, and keep me safe when a worry appeared. I really wanted to tell everyone about the safe place that He represents, and the peace He has always so faithfully given to me, but I also wanted to be normal.   Really. Normal. Like anyone is really normal.   But that was the place I found comfort. Love Jesus. Be normal.

Then one day....BAM....I stumbled into God in a new way. This book is the result of my recent encounter with the One who breathed out the stars, decided the ocean depths, hid diamonds in the mountains, and placed you in your mom's belly. I found out something amazing about Him: He is right next to me, He is always thinking about me, and He loves me fiercely.   Sometimes, when I am really coming close to His heart, I can almost feel his breath on my face. He knows my every thought. He loves me, even when I am making a mess of life and his commands.   If I will let Him...if I will ask Him....He has so much to tell me about one of my favorite subjects...me.

He wants you to know Him this way, too. He loves you like this. The Bible says it in many places. In James' letter, the Bible says "you don't have what you want because you don't ask for it" (James 4:2). Elsewhere, Jesus says "ask and you will receive, knock and the door will be opened."   It never occurred to me that He was talking about receiving more of Him.   He wants me to have more fascination with Him, because He is fascinated with me! Does that surprise you? It shouldn't. Jesus is fascinated with you, too! In fact, that is why I am writing to you. I want to send you down the road knowing a little bit more of how Jesus feels about you, and in the process, I want to tell you about some of His plans for the near future because they include you.

You really don't know how important you are, but I am hoping to get you started in discovering it. You will have to decide if you will take it from there. You don't have to. He won't force you. He'll still love you either way. Love is why He leaves the start of the conversation for you. He's chosen you, but you have to choose Him. If you begin asking Him to talk with you more, He will blow you away with what He has to say. I mean really asking Him, though. Not just a onetime "hey Jesus, please tell me about me." I mean asking like you mean it. The same way you would bug your mom and dad to go see that movie you really want to see. Or like you would bug your brother or sister to change the channel to a show you really want to watch. Jesus really wants to talk to you, but it is up to you to ask and keep asking until you hear him in your heart. Does this sound too good to be true? It is so simple anyone can ask God for this, but so simple almost no one does. This is my story: I asked, and I received. What He had to show me once I started the conversation has changed my life forever. So I continue to ask, and I continue to receive. I want to keep reaching, so I can keep growing. It is that simple. You have some time to mull it over, a little time anyway. I'll get started while you are deciding.

I have made a couple of assumptions about you: First, I am assuming you are a teenager, or at least willing to be a teenager at heart. When Jesus told me to write this I realized He was asking me to send a message to teenagers who's ages were in the general ballpark of my sons (we'll say 10-18). My boys, my wife Samantha, and I talk about this stuff a lot. I figure Jesus gave me this assignment because He knows I like talking to young people about God. It is one of my favorite things in life. I really like talking about God, and teenagers are willing to listen and talk more than most people realize. Plus, you are smarter and more aware than almost anyone realizes.

Second, I am assuming you already believe a couple of things: 1. That the Bible is true. Without us having this in common, the stuff I am going to tell you will make no sense.

2. That you know Jesus is the actual one and only Son of God the Father, that He paid the price for your mistakes (sins) when He died on the cross, and that He rose again from the dead. Basically, I am assuming you know Jesus as your Savior. If you aren't sure, it is as easy as telling God that you know these things (what I listed in #2) are true, asking God to forgive you for your mistakes because of what Jesus did on the cross, and then committing to give leadership of your life to Jesus to the best of your ability. You can do this out loud, right now. God can hear you no matter where you are. If you just told God that, I want you to put this book down, go tell someone about it, and then come back and we'll start up where we left off.

Love: The Ultimate Battle Plan - 2

"No one saves the best for last." These were the first words spoken when Jesus introduced people to his first miracle. He had just turned water into wine at a wedding. The guests were astounded at how good it was. This is Jesus' way, though. They shouldn't have been surprised when Jesus gave them the best when they least expected it. He is always doing stuff like that. I want you to catch this: He has saved the best for last, and you are going to be blown away. The world would want you to think otherwise, but I know the truth!

Once I began understanding the main story line, things I was seeing in the news started to make a lot more sense. I can see what the Bible described beginning to happen all around me. Once you hear Jesus' plans, if you watch even a little bit of the news, you will start to see where we are heading. When I say beginning to happen, I really mean the beginning of the end. If world history was an action movie, we would be getting to the last chase scene just before the big finale. As I study the sequence of the story, the more I can see it playing out. As I see it playing out, the more I realize you and I (the Church) have a main role in this drama. As my role becomes clearer, I realize I have to share the story with as many people as I can!

The basic plot is this: Jesus has a plan to drive evil off the planet and establish a whole new government. This new government won't be like anything you can imagine. It will literally be a whole governmental system that is based on His love. His love is perfect, so this government will be perfect too. Can you imagine a perfectly loving postman? Or a perfectly loving policeman? How about a perfectly loving and truthful President or Congressman? I know, right now that seems like a stretch, but trust me, that is just the icing on the cake.

Our Current Opposition

For this new loving world government to begin, the Bible says this current age, the one dominated by sin, and greed, and self interest, has to come to an end. You have probably heard people talk about the end of the world. When you hear about the end of world, or Armageddon, or the apocalypse, what do you picture? It amazes me how the "worldly" ideas about what is going to happen in the future subtly try to invade our lives. The "world" really doesn't want you to know the truth about what Jesus is doing. I say the "world" because I can't think of any one person in particular who is trying to keep the truth from us, but the "world system" really seems to hide the truth. There *is* a Biblical reason for this: In the book of Ephesians, the apostle Paul said that here on earth, people, in this instance "people" would be the media (people who make movies, television, internet), are not our enemy. It is easy to think there is some sort of human conspiracy to keep us from knowing the truth, but check out Ephesians 6:12:

> *(Ephesians 6:12) For we are not fighting against flesh-and-blood enemies, but against evil rulers and authorities of the unseen world, against mighty powers in this dark world, and against evil spirits in the heavenly places.*

So who are these evil rulers and authorities of the unseen world...the mighty powers in this dark world....the evil spirits in the heavenly places? I'll level with you: Paul was talking about the devil and the angels that rebelled against God with the devil. They are enemies of God, and therefore they are our enemies, too. Paul was face-to-face with these enemies a lot. We don't hear much about them anymore, but they are very real. You might also hear them called satan and his demons. Check out what the Bible says satan did when he rebelled against God, you will find it in Revelation 12:4:

> *(Revelation 12:4) His tail swept away one-third of the stars in the sky, and he threw them to the earth. He stood in front of the woman as she was about to give birth, ready to devour her baby as soon as it was born.*

There is a little bit of symbolism here, but it is easy to figure out from the rest of the passage that the dragon is satan, and the stars that were thrown to earth are fallen angels, or demons. The Bible says that these bad apples have access to heaven and earth. That is until our King of Kings, Jesus, comes and takes care of them once and for all. Until then, they roam around like a lion, looking for ways to separate people from each other, and from God. Now, before you get too worked up and lose sleep worrying about invisible demons roaming around, there are a few things you need to know about these enemies of ours:

1.   Their power is almost completely limited to their ability to lie to you, and in you believing their lies. Not every thought in your head comes from you. Some come from you, some

from the Holy Spirit, and some from the enemies (imagine when you are tempted in your mind to do something you know you shouldn't or don't want to do, often these thoughts are lies from your enemy).

2.   Although they are almost completely limited to lying, demons can cause some sickness and other problems (read 2 Corinthians 12:7. Not all sickness is demon-related, but sometimes it is...not to worry, see #3)

3.   Jesus crushed all of satan's authority. Their legal right to mess with you (yes, heaven is governed by laws) was taken away from them when Jesus paid the price for our sins on the cross. Satan and his demons are still law breakers and try to mess with you, but if you resist them, they have to go (James 4:7). The Bible describes how you can not only prevent demonic access to you (binding), but how you can start freeing others (interceding) from their dark deception and trouble (Chapter 6, if you are the type to skip ahead).

4.   Right now, the enemy is scared. Their time of destruction is quickly approaching.

5.   The enemies of God are really scared of YOU. They are worried that if you find out who you are in Jesus' eyes, and who they really are, they

will lose their illegal grip on the world. Again, you are WAY more important than you know.

6.   Satan and his demon's time is just about up, so they are really trying to avoid their prison sentence. This is the key to understanding what is happening in the world right now.

When we start to think about the "end of the world" (the world is NOT going to end, by the way) we have to realize that a lot of the thoughts about this (Mayan Calendar predictions, large meteors hitting the earth, global warming, etc.) are deceptions from these "evil rulers" designed to distract us from the real story. The real story is found in the Book of Truth, the Bible. God put everything we need to know about His plans in the Bible.   If something isn't in the Bible, we really don't want to give it space in our hearts or minds.

Who owns the Earth?

The enemy casts so much doubt on the Bible because he knows when you start to see what the Word really says about this time, you will begin to take an active role in Jesus' battle plans, and then the enemy's life is that much harder. So for right now, I want you to throw away everything you think you know about the end of the age (that is what we will call it, since this is the most accurate way to describe it: the end of the age of sin, and the beginning of the age of righteousness!). I am going to briefly catch you up on the earth's chain-of-title (the legal trail of who owns the earth). (I am giving you verses so you can see who owned the authority over the earth, and when it transfers. This is really important. I recommend you take a couple of minutes to look these up in your own Bible so you can be confident about this truth):

God creates earth (and the rest of the universe)

God creates Adam and Eve

God gives earth to Adam and Eve to rule over (or govern) in partnership with God (Genesis 1:28)

Adam and Eve rebel against God by believing satan instead of God, and they do the one thing they were not supposed to do (eat from the Tree of Knowledge of Good and Evil)

God really gave the earth to Adam and Eve, so when they rebelled against God, they really gave their ownership of the earth (or *authority* over the earth) to satan (Luke 4:6)

God knew this would happen (He knows everything) and had already planned to send His son Jesus, as a perfect man, to redeem (buy back) the ownership of the earth for mankind (God was serious about giving the earth to man). Jesus defeated satan at the cross, and now has authority over all things (Matthew 28:18)

Satan, the ultimate thief and liar, continues to pretend to be an authority on earth. He knows a prison sentence hangs over his head, but Jesus made some promises about His return that satan, in his blinding pride, thinks he can use to avoid prison

Ok…here we are in the present time…

What Time is it and What is Next?

There are a lot of prophecies in the Bible that help us know where we are at in God's timeline, and what still has to happen. A couple of big prophecies mark the time we are in now. They are the creation of the country of Israel overnight (Isaiah 66:8), and the coming of a person, a man, known as the antichrist. One of these prophecies has been fulfilled, and one hasn't yet. Look at what it says in Daniel 9:26-27? I'm going to ask you to pause in the middle of reading it to show you where we are at:

> *(Daniel 9:26-27) "After this period of sixty-two sets of seven, the Anointed One will be killed, appearing to have accomplished nothing, and a ruler will arise whose armies will destroy the city and the Temple.* ***PAUSE*** *The end will come with a flood, and war and its miseries are decreed from that time to the very end. The ruler will make a treaty with the people for a period of one set of seven, but after half this time, he will put an end to the sacrifices and offerings. And as a climax to all his terrible deeds, he will set up a sacrilegious object that causes desecration, until the fate decreed for this defiler is finally poured out on him."*

We are right in the spot where I wrote "pause". Jesus is the Anointed One. He came, and He was killed. The Jewish people, who the prophet Daniel was talking to, thought Jesus accomplished nothing (they did not accept Jesus as the promised Messiah or Savior), but we know Jesus saved mankind through His death. Then the next part comes. This is what the angel talking to Daniel called "the end." The angel talks about an evil ruler who makes peace for Israel. What you guys might not know is that Israel was destroyed, just like the angel told Daniel in Chapter 9, and then for over 1800 years (70 A.D. until 1948), there was no country of Israel, and no Jewish temple in Israel.

All of the prophecies about Jesus' return, and there are a lot, require Israel to be a nation, and for a temple to be located in Jerusalem. Israel became a nation, literally overnight, in 1948. At the end of World War II, the country of Israel was created by some men signing some papers. The prophet Isaiah said it would happen overnight in Isaiah 66:8. Since then, Israel has been fighting to have control over Jerusalem. Israel really wants to build a temple in Jerusalem. The next prophecy we are waiting to be fulfilled is for this world ruler, who the Bible calls the antichrist, to make peace in the middle east, and for Israel to build the temple the Bible talks about.

People hear the name "antichrist" and they think many different things. Maybe they picture the devil in a suit, or a crazy madman, or someone with a wicked laugh, but He is just a man. He is a world ruler, like a president or a king, who will come to power and seem like a really good guy. He will make peace in the middle east, where many people are fighting. In fact, He will make a 7-year treaty between Israel and all the people who want to destroy Israel. Sometime between now and 3 ½ years after the antichrist makes this peace treaty, Israel will build the temple in Jerusalem. Then, something super important happens. Look at Daniel 12:11:

(Daniel 12:11) "From the time the daily sacrifice is stopped and the sacrilegious object that causes desecration is set up to be worshiped, there will be 1,290 days.

This is important because the angel told Daniel that the antichrist will setup a statue in the temple that He will want everyone to worship (the sacrilegious object). Then the antichrist will say he is god, and he wants everyone to worship Him instead of the real God of Abraham, Isaac, and Jacob. After that happens, it will be 3 ½ years until Jesus comes and destroys the antichrist.

These 3 ½ years will be a troubling time for the earth. During those 3 ½ years, Jesus will punish the antichrist, and the people who worship Him, to show people they are wrong about God. He will do this in order to get rid of the things that keep people from knowing and loving God. God's whole point in creating mankind was to be with us (read John 17 sometime). When the antichrist begins trying to force people to worship him as god, some people will choose to worship the antichrist because it will make sense to them. Some people, like us, will stay true to Jesus and will be a witness to others that Jesus is the Way, the Truth, and the Life. We are promised in the Bible a "great harvest" of those who will come to know Jesus as Savior at this time (Revelation 7:9). Some people will resist both Jesus (and our witness of Him as Savior) and the antichrist. This will leave the world in great turmoil. The prophet Joel called it the "Great and Terrible" day of the Lord (Joel 2:31). It is during this time that Jesus will judge the antichrist empire to save as many people as possible, with the least amount of destruction possible.

The judgments that Jesus will use will get stronger and stronger. Jesus uses the least intense means possible to show people that He judges everything that gets in the way of love. Everything Jesus does is to redeem (that just means to buy back) the people He loves. Jesus really wants people to choose Him for salvation. He knows that being separated from Jesus for eternity in Hell is way worse than even the judgments He will send on the antichrist and his followers.

The judgments are really important for us to understand, because God will release them through us. The Bible tells us exactly what the judgments will be, and what order they will be released in. God numbered and ordered them, and put them in the Bible, so we would know exactly what was happening, and who was in charge (obviously I mean God!). As I said earlier, the judgments go from less severe to more severe. You can think about it like this: When your mom and dad tell you to do something and you choose not to listen, you probably get in trouble. Do you get in the most trouble right away, or do you get a warning first, then more severe punishment after? When a parent loves us, they always try to punish us in the least severe way to still get the necessary result. God really loves people, even people that are rebelling against Him. His punishments go from easiest to worst, because He really wants people to come into agreement with Him, and experience His love.

Exodus...again

When we start to read about the judgments in the book of Revelation, they can seem very frightening if we don't understand God's intentions. It is important that we know the judgments are for people rebelling against God, not for those in agreement with Him. Jesus doesn't want anyone to go to

Hell (Matthew 18:14).   While people who know Jesus will experience living in a world in turmoil, the judgments are not directed at them. In fact, God will protect His people from the judgments.   Check out what it says in Revelation 7:3:

> *(Revelation 7:3) "Wait! Don't harm the land or the sea or the trees until we have placed the seal of God on the foreheads of His servants."*

We can trust God.   Not only does He promise to protect people that are in agreement with Him, He has proven time and time again that this is how He operates (one example can be found in Genesis 18:17-33). A great example of God's heart in a time of judgment is the story of Moses leading the Israelites out of Egypt in the book of Exodus. You can read about it in Exodus 9. Understanding the Exodus story is a key to understanding the book of Revelation. Exodus is an account of the saving of the nation of Israel from the evil government of Pharaoh. Revelation is the saving of the entire Church from the evil government of satan. Revelation 15:3-4 is a great key in understanding the relationship between the Exodus of Israel and the Exodus of the Church at the time of Jesus' return. It describes the "Song of Moses" the seven angels who will release the seven last plagues of Revelation will be singing. What an amazing connection God draws for us here.

Understanding the relationship between the Exodus story and Revelation is so important. God sent His servant Moses to tell Pharaoh to let the Israelites go. Pharaoh didn't like being told what to do, and he really liked having the Israelites as slaves, so he told Moses, and God, no. God began releasing judgment, in the form of plagues, on Egypt. It is no coincidence that many of the plagues described in the book of Exodus are the same as the judgments described in Revelation. God says He never changes (James 1:17). When God released judgments in Egypt, He protected the Israelites. Check out what it says in Exodus 9:6:

> *(Exodus 9:6) And the LORD did just as He had said. The next morning all the livestock of the Egyptians died, but the Israelites didn't lose a single animal.*

And how about Exodus 9:26:

> *(Exodus 9:26) The only place without hail was the region of Goshen, where the people of Israel lived.*

The plagues that God released in Egypt did not harm the Israelites. The Israelites were not rebelling against God; Pharaoh and the Egyptians were. Although the Israelites still had to live in a place of turmoil, they were protected from the really scary stuff. God's intention to protect His people from judgment is essential to understand, but to get insight into what our role in Jesus' plan will be we have to draw one more connection between the Exodus story and Revelation. God did not just send the plagues on Egypt, He released them through Moses! It was Moses' job to tell Pharaoh what God wanted him to do, to warn the Egyptians. If the Egyptians would have come into agreement with God, no plague would have been necessary. But, if the Egyptians rebelled against God, then, at God's direction, Moses released the plagues. The Bible says Moses released them by praying for them to come, or speaking them out in obedience to God's plan.

The same thing will be true when Jesus judges the antichrist's empire. The victorious Church, under persecution, but walking in the great power of the Holy Spirit (think Book of Acts, but with a lot more miracles!) will be telling people to turn to Jesus so they can be saved. The Church will warn a confused world of the coming judgments. As people come into agreement with God and accept Jesus as Savior, they will come into God's protection. However, the Bible says many people will harden their hearts against God. When this happens, the Church will be releasing the judgments through prayer in agreement with Jesus' plan.

Glance through Revelation 6, 8, 9, 15, and 16 (seriously, you should do this right now!) Look at the organization of the judgments. They are numbered and organized, and written out in order. We know 3 always comes after 2, right?! Well in the days when Jesus releases His judgments, His whole Church will know exactly what to pray for. We will all be in agreement. The Chapters 6 through 16 in the book of Revelation are the Church's prayer manual to be in agreement with Jesus, like Moses was working with God in the book of Exodus. But get this, instead of God revealing His plans to one man, like Moses; God has revealed His plan to the whole Church. The whole Church will get to share in Jesus' awesome plan to remove evil from the earth.

Satan's Fear

We have just spent time looking at Jesus' plan from the perspective of the Church. But there is another side to this story. Actually, it is satan's schemes we watch playing out in world history. Satan has his own plan to avoid the punishment Jesus promised was coming to him. Satan's plan really hinges on Jesus' truthfulness and faithfulness. You see,

Jesus made some promises about His plans that satan thinks he can use to his own advantage. Check out what Jesus said in Matthew 23:37-39:

> *(Matthew 23:37-39) "O Jerusalem, Jerusalem, the city that kills the prophets and stones God's messengers! How often I have wanted to gather your children together as a hen protects her chicks beneath her wings, but you wouldn't let Me.   And now, look, your house is abandoned and desolate.   For I tell you this, you will never see Me again until you say, 'Blessings on the One who comes in the name of the LORD!'"*

Jesus said this shortly before He went to the cross. What did He promise Jerusalem? He said basically, "you won't see me again until you invite me back." The people of Israel rejected Jesus as the promised Messiah, but the Bible is clear that someday Israel will realize Jesus is really the Messiah. This was Jesus' promise in Matthew 23:39: I am coming back, but not until you invite me as the One who comes in the name of the Lord, another name for the Messiah (Psalm 118:26).

The devil thinks this promise that Jesus made gives him and his demons a potential loophole to avoid prison. By keeping Jewish people in Jerusalem from inviting Jesus back as Messiah, satan and his helpers hope to avoid the destruction promised to them. They know God will not lie. If you look at the history of Jerusalem, and the Jewish people, since the time Jesus made this promise, satan's strategy becomes clearer.

As I mentioned before, shortly after Jesus went to the cross, the entire state of Israel, including the City of Jerusalem, was destroyed by the Romans. For over 1800 years, the Jewish people lived scattered across the world, without a true homeland.   Persecution and attempted elimination of the Jews has occurred numerous times since 100 A.D.   Notable attempts of satan's to wipe out the Jewish people include attacks on Jews during the Crusades (around 1000 A.D.) and the Nazi holocaust from 1941 through 1945 (where 6,000,000 Jewish people were killed).

Satan's strategy is even more pronounced if you look at the City of Jerusalem.   Ever since the city was destroyed by the Romans in 70 A.D., control of Jerusalem has been the source of nearly constant struggle.   When the state of Israel was formed in 1948, control of Jerusalem was not given to Israel.   What is known as the Six Day War, which occurred in 1967, resulted in Israel gaining control over a large portion of Jerusalem.   However, in order to try and maintain peace with its Muslim neighbors, Israel has let Islamic leaders control the Temple Mount (or the place where the Temple must be located according to Jewish rules) in Israel.   Because of this, Jewish people cannot use the Temple Mount, let alone build a new temple there.   The Temple Mount is a place of extreme political tension, because both Muslims and Jews have very special feelings about the holiness of the site.   Primarily because of this issue, there has not been peace in the middle east for a long time.   This is one of the many reasons it is so important for us to pray for the protection of Israel, Jerusalem, and the Jewish people.

Remember what Paul said in Ephesians 6?   What the world sees as fighting between the Jewish people and the others who don't want Israel to control Jerusalem is really the "evil rulers and authorities of the unseen world" trying to keep a Jewish city called Jerusalem from inviting Jesus back as its Messiah.   Jerusalem is constantly in the news today, as peace in the middle east has become a focal point of world politics.

The Bible predicted all this would happen, and as surely as winter turns to spring, someday soon, a world ruler will produce a peace treaty that will allow a temple to be built in Jerusalem. Satan's very efforts to survive will include building the temple the prophet Daniel predicted would mark the unfolding of Jesus' plans to drive satan off the planet. Talk about irony!

The Babylon Connection

If you have stayed with me this long, you might be wondering "how is satan's plan to build a temple going to help him stay out of prison?" Satan knows that ultimately he has to keep the Jewish people in Jerusalem from knowing and worshipping Jesus as Messiah. If you study the book of Revelation a little bit, and then combine it with other prophecies concerning the end of the age (check out Daniel 11:36-39), you quickly realize that satan intends to setup a whole new false religion, called in the Bible the "Mystery Babylon."

Babylon is a place, and for us to know why it becomes important at the end of the age, we need to look at the first mention of Babylon in the Bible. Check out what it says about Babylon in Genesis 11:

> (Genesis 11:1-11) At one time all the people of the world spoke the same language and used the same words. As the people migrated to the east, they found a plain in the land of Babylonia and settled there. They began saying to each other, "Let's make bricks and harden them with fire." (In this region bricks were used instead of stone, and tar was used for mortar.) Then they said, "Come, let's build a great city for

ourselves with a tower that reaches into the sky. This will make us famous and keep us from being scattered all over the world." But the LORD came down to look at the city and the tower the people were building. "Look!" He said. "The people are united, and they all speak the same language. After this, nothing they set out to do will be impossible for them! Come, let's go down and confuse the people with different languages. Then they won't be able to understand each other." In that way, the LORD scattered them all over the world, and they stopped building the city.

When you read that story, you might be left with the impression God was worried the people in Babylon would build a tower all the way to heaven. Think about that for a minute. Would God, who created everything, be worried about a bunch of people setting up a really tall building? No way! God was saying the people at that time were completely united, and nothing was slowing them down from collaborating with each other. There was no language barrier, and they were intent on following their sinful hearts. God knows the heart of man is sinful. Without Jesus, people are really messed up. You see the news, and you know what I am talking about. God wasn't ready for the earth to experience the fullness of evil that happens when people take what is in their heart to the extreme. To delay this development of a united force of humans working after one collective goal (which, because of man's sinful heart, would necessarily have to be evil, apart from God) God gave people different languages.

Up until recently, the differences in human language were very hard to overcome. Groups of people that spoke different languages didn't communicate frequently. But think about what has happened in the last 10 years. What has made communication increase dramatically? Yes! The internet has changed everything! For the first time since the Tower of Babylon, people can really come together for good, or for evil. Think about the number of horrible things you may accidentally see or read by searching for an innocent word on the internet. The web is a mine-field littered with evidence of the evil desires in the hearts of people. When a lot of evil minded people from all over the world are able to collaborate with each other, really bad stuff comes out of it. The internet is a MAJOR force in the world.

This Mystery Babylon religion will be the ultimate expression of what God delayed in Babylon back in Genesis 11. People will celebrate it as a religion bringing peace and goodwill to earth. Fairness will be its selling point, and this religion will sound really kind and good. It will be accepted by people of many faiths, and it will tolerate many religions...except one. Can you guess who the Mystery Babylon will reject? Yes, this religion that is supposed to be tolerant of all faiths will reject dedication to Jesus. The Babylon religion might be willing to tolerate the name of Jesus, but it will fight against anyone who claims Jesus is the only way to God. The Mystery Babylon will promise the peace, and justice, and fairness only the true Prince of Peace, Jesus, can deliver. Mystery Babylon will be an anti-Jesus religion, and will eventually be hijacked by the antichrist himself.

Satan's Strategy

This is where all of the information I have been giving you comes together. When the antichrist hijacks this Mystery

Babylon religion, he will then declare himself to be god. He will suddenly become intolerant of any religion except the worship of himself. Then he will command the Jewish people to stop the sacrifices and worship in their new temple, that he allowed them to build by way of his peace treaty, and he will try to force people to choose him as a god. Check out what the angel told the prophet Daniel about the antichrist:

> *(Daniel 11:31) "His army will take over the Temple fortress, pollute the sanctuary, put a stop to the daily sacrifices, and set up the sacrilegious object that causes desecration. He will flatter and win over those who have violated the covenant. But the people who know their God will be strong and will resist him.*

The antichrist will be so motivated to get people to worship him (and prevent them from inviting Jesus back as Messiah) that he will setup an economic system that will prevent people who do not worship him from being able to buy or sell stuff. If you have ever heard of the mark of the beast, that describes one aspect of the antichrist economic system. Just like we might use credit cards today, someday in the future there will be a way to buy and sell things using a mark on your hand or your head (Rev 13:17).

This is all the result of satan's desire to stay out of prison. First, the devil tried to get rid of the Jewish people all together. Then he tried to keep them from living in Jerusalem. As a last ditch effort, he will try to trick Israel into cooperating with his Mystery Babylon religion by letting them build the temple they have wanted for centuries. Then, when satan thinks he has Israel right where he wants her, he will try to force her, through fear and intimidation, into worshipping him instead of God. His pride is blinding him to the fact that God will win, and the end of the story will be exactly as God has written it out.

Jesus will be victorious in not only judging everything that gets in the way of His love for us, but He will decisively beat the antichrist and lock up satan. Jesus' plans all come to a boil as He marches into Jerusalem with His victorious Church The Church will finally be the "Pure and Spotless bride" who has made herself ready (Rev 19:7) in a time of trouble. As we march with Him into Jerusalem, Jesus meets the antichrist face to face. This is the big finale, when Jesus destroys the antichrist, and throws the devil in prison. Check out what it says in 2 Thessalonians 2:8:

> *(2 Thessalonians 2:8) Then the man of lawlessness will be revealed, but the Lord Jesus will kill him with the breath of His mouth and destroy him by the splendor of His coming.*

This verse describes the big showdown, Jesus versus the evil world ruler, and poof...Jesus reveals His glory, blows on the antichrist, and the antichrist is defeated! Jesus is so powerful. He is perfectly powerful **and** perfectly loving. He knows exactly what He is doing, and He told us His plans in advance. Can you imagine that? Jesus is so confident of His plans. He actually tells the whole world what His plans are. No military general would dare tell his enemy what his plans are, but Jesus laid His all out for the world to see, because He knows nothing can stop Him!

The Ancient Highway - 3

The Bible says that as the time for Jesus' return gets closer, the world will get darker, but the light will also get brighter. When you think about the place you live, do things seem to be going well, or do there seem to be a lot of problems?   When you watch the news, does it seem like people know how to fix our problems, or do they just argue about whose fault it is? Does it matter for you? Whether the debt piles up in our government, or the TV shows get raunchier and raunchier, does it really matter for you? How about riots in other countries and protests here, can you do anything about it? Is it related to Jesus' plan to return, or is it just another cycle that will turn back the other way given enough time? Will the problems in our world just take care of themselves? I want you to read what God said through the prophet Jeremiah when his country of Israel was in a similar moment in time:

> *(Jeremiah 18:15-16) But My people are not so reliable, for they have deserted Me; they burn incense to worthless idols. They have stumbled off the ancient highways and walk in muddy paths. Therefore, their land will become desolate, a monument to their stupidity. All who pass by will be astonished and will shake their heads in amazement.*

The verse I quoted above is God's statement about the nation of Israel shortly before He judged them by sending the Babylonian army to completely destroy the city of Jerusalem.

The prophet Jeremiah was sent to warn his friends and neighbors, people he didn't know, and even some who hated him, about the impending destruction. When you think about the USA, God's statement through Jeremiah is a little sobering. He said of Israel "they have stumbled off the ancient highways and walk in muddy paths." God is so good at creating a visual message. What is a highway for? It gets you where you want to go, fast. How about a muddy path? Have you ever walked down a muddy trail? It is rough walking. Your feet can't find a stable place to land, it's messy, it's uncomfortable, and it's slow. When God called the highway "ancient", He was saying "this highway has been around a long time. You know it works to get you where you want to go, and you know it gets you there fast." Can you hear God's dismay that the Israelites would choose the muddy path over the ancient highways?

The ancient highway God was describing was Himself, and being in a right relationship with Him. He was saying "you Israelites have abandoned Me, the ONE THING you had going for you." The same thing can be said about us. Think about our country for just a minute. It was founded on God. The Pilgrims originally came here to be able to worship freely. Although we have struggled off and on, we are widely recognized as one of the most successful countries....ever. For over a century, people from other countries have made countless sacrifices just to get into our country. The opportunities available to Americans are unique.

As America removes God from our schools and other public institutions, we watch things in our country get worse. The downfall of our financial well being, our influence in the world, and our moral standing coincide with this constant attempt to remove God from every part of our government.

America isn't the only nation to ever experience this. Ancient Israel also walked down this path. God always warns us, like He did through Jeremiah.

God is so merciful. The Bible says He is slow to get angry and quick to forgive. Look at what the prophet Jonah said:

> *(Jonah 4:2) So he complained to the LORD about it: "Didn't I say before I left home that You would do this, LORD? That is why I ran away to Tarshish! I knew that You are a merciful and compassionate God, slow to get angry and filled with unfailing love. You are eager to turn back from destroying people.*

Jonah had just been sent to Nineveh, another country going in the same direction we are heading, to announce God's impending judgment of the city. The Ninevite king repented as soon as he heard the message Jonah was to deliver. Look at what the king of Nineveh said:

> *(Jonah 3:9) Who can tell? Perhaps even yet God will change His mind and hold back His fierce anger from destroying us."*

The Joel Solution

So what are we supposed to do when things get bad because we have wandered off the ancient highway? God gives the answer in several places in the Bible, but I bet you don't even need to hear it to know what it is: Get back on the highway and out of the mud! The prophet Joel said it like this:

(Joel 2:12)   That is why the LORD says, "Turn to Me now, while there is time. Give Me your hearts. Come with fasting, weeping, and mourning.   Don't tear your clothing in your grief, but tear your hearts instead." Return to the LORD your God, for He is merciful and compassionate, slow to get angry and filled with unfailing love. He is eager to relent and not punish. Who knows? Perhaps He will give you a reprieve, sending you a blessing instead of this curse. Perhaps you will be able to offer grain and wine to the LORD your God as before.

The problems our world faces right now are nothing new in the great scheme of things. The world has turned away from God, and we are experiencing the consequences of turning away from Him. Joel was describing the end of the age. You know from Chapter 1 that it is my belief we are at the beginning of the time period Joel was describing. Interestingly, the last verse in that passage from Joel is saying the same thing the King of Nineveh said: Who knows? Maybe God will change His mind about where I live.

A man named Abraham asked this same question when a town near him was about to be judged. Abraham lived near a town called Sodom. This place was really evil. The people were cruel and uncaring.   The Lord had determined to destroy the city, but before He destroyed it He visited with Abraham. You can read about it in Genesis 18. I want you to look at the conversation between Abraham and the Lord:

(Gen 18:22-33)   The other men turned and headed toward Sodom, but the LORD remained with Abraham.

Abraham approached Him and said, "Will You sweep away both the righteous and the wicked?   Suppose You find fifty righteous people living there in the city— will You still sweep it away and not spare it for their sakes? Surely You wouldn't do such a thing, destroying the righteous along with the wicked. Why, You would be treating the righteous and the wicked exactly the same! Surely You wouldn't do that! Should not the Judge of all the earth do what is right?"

And the LORD replied, "If I find fifty righteous people in Sodom, I will spare the entire city for their sake."   Then Abraham spoke again. "Since I have begun, let me speak further to my Lord, even though I am but dust and ashes. Suppose there are only forty-five righteous people rather than fifty? Will You destroy the whole city for lack of five?" And the LORD said, "I will not destroy it if I find forty-five righteous people there." Then Abraham pressed his request further. "Suppose there are only forty?" And the LORD replied, "I will not destroy it for the sake of the forty."

"Please don't be angry, my Lord," Abraham pleaded. "Let me speak—suppose only thirty righteous people are found?" And the LORD replied, "I will not destroy it if I find thirty."   Then Abraham said, "Since I have dared to speak to the Lord, let me continue—suppose there are only twenty?" And the LORD replied, "Then I will not destroy it for the sake of the twenty."   Finally, Abraham said, "Lord, please don't be angry with me if I speak one more time. Suppose only ten are found

*there?" And the LORD replied, "Then I will not destroy it
for the sake of the ten."*

Sodom was destroyed a few days after Abraham had
this conversation with the Lord.   God spared Abraham's
nephew, Lot, but the rest of the inhabitants of Sodom were
destroyed with the city. God could not find even 10 righteous
people in Sodom. Could you imagine if nine other righteous
(that just means in a right relationship with God) people
would have been found in Sodom? God promised the WHOLE
city would have been spared.

How can WE protect OUR city?

So this is the question: as Jesus' plans unfold for the
end of the age, and judgment begins to be poured out on the
earth, how many righteous people would it take for God to
spare your city? Could you be the person responsible for
making the place you live a "land of Goshen," the place God's
people were protected from the judgments in the book of
Exodus? If you listen to God's warnings before the coming
judgments in each of these stories: Jeremiah, Joel, Nineveh,
and Sodom, you would quickly see the formula for mercy for a
geographic region is found in the decisions of individual
people, like YOU!

I want to turn your attention back to what the prophet
Joel said in Joel 2:12: *That is why the LORD says, "Turn to Me
now, while there is time. Give Me your hearts. Come with
fasting, weeping, and mourning. Don't tear your clothing in
your grief, but tear your hearts instead."* I want you to read
those words a couple of times out loud. When you hear
those words, what does it make you think about God? Does it
leave you with the impression He is hoping to destroy some

people, or that He really loves people? He isn't saying "you have to earn your way back into my good graces," is He? No. He is saying, "I love you. I made you to be with me. You have wandered away. Give your heart back to me." God knows that when trouble is on the horizon, He is the only safe place. This message is for people that already know God AND those who don't.

This is the crazy thing: Giving our whole hearts to God is so worth it, regardless of what judgment may be coming. We really shouldn't need to be convinced to turn back to God with our whole hearts. Jesus said when you give everything you have to God (you make Him the most important thing in your life), you get a full life in return (John 10:10). All of the stuff we try to hang onto, because we think it will make our lives better, actually keeps us from the full life God WANTS to give us. However, if we will let go of all that "stuff" and cling only to God, He promises to give us all we need, and want, for a full life.

Our misunderstanding of how to have the "good life" gets in the way of turning all our desire towards God.   The truth of how God's economy really works makes no sense from the world's point of view. According to human "common sense" if you want more money, you work harder and save more money. You try hard to keep more in your hands. According to God's wisdom, if you want more money, you risk it by giving it to other people who need it and using it to help others whenever you see God opening a door. According to human common sense, if you want more time, you don't agree to help other people out in ways that take up your time. In God's economy, if you want more time, you sacrifice the time you have to help others. According to the human way of doing things, if you want more possessions, you don't loan them to others. You save them only for you and take such good care of them they look like they have never been used. In God's wisdom, if you want more possessions, or to really be able to enjoy your possessions, you share with anyone who asks, with no conditions, and you trust God to preserve your stuff according to His wisdom.

These ideas are the exact opposites of what most people say to do. Even around most Christians in America, if you act this way you will appear extreme. This isn't extreme, this is simply obeying what Jesus says is true. God really cares that you have the right amounts of time, money, and possessions to carry out His plans for your life, but ultimately, His plan is that you would have MORE OF GOD in your life, and He would have your whole heart.

Once you experience His presence and miraculous provision, you would trade ALL of your money, time, and "stuff" for more of God! Once you realize He is in control of all the stuff, this turns out to be the best deal in the entire universe. If I tried to hang onto all those things the world tells me to keep for myself, I might have a little more than I started with, and I might not, but I would have missed out on the whole point of life: to know God more. He created us to be with Him.

Wholeheartedness Changes Everything!

So what does it mean to give God your whole heart? Jesus had a lot to say about this. In fact, Jesus gave a whole sermon, called the Sermon on the Mount, about this exact thing. Every time the Bible records someone asking Jesus what the most important commandment to obey was, Jesus gave the same answer: Love the Lord your God with all your heart, with all your soul, and with all your mind! (Matthew

22:36). It is important we get a handle on exactly what Jesus is describing.

When you think of loving God with your whole heart, what comes to mind? Praying all day? Reading the Bible for several hours a day? Not having too much fun? Not watching anything "bad" on tv? Giving up video games or movies? Walking away from friends who make bad choices?

Before I learned about "wholeheartedness" I always thought loving God with my whole heart meant having more discipline to do "Christian" things, and more discipline to not do "non-Christian" things. I was WAY wrong. I had the whole idea exactly backwards. I thought that doing, or not doing, certain things I associated with "good Christians", things like reading my Bible more, or praying more, or serving more, would make my heart closer to God. The truth is, getting your heart closer to God will make you do those things more! Let's look at the two approaches like a math problem:

Me + Bible Reading + Praying + Serving = More God

Or

Me + More God = Bible Reading + Praying + Serving

There is a HUGE difference between the two equations. The first one looks really Christian but is really hard to keep going for very long. Maintaining this is hard because without a close relationship with God, the reading, praying, and serving can get really boring, quick. If you have ever decided "I am going to read my Bible every day from now on" you probably know what I am talking about. At first, the fact that we made a commitment will drive us. Learning more about God might be interesting for a while, but we quickly get distracted, or bored, or burned out. Humans generally stink at discipline.

If you are a person with a lot of natural discipline, it can go even worse for you. You might decide to read your Bible more, and have the strength to stick with it. But quickly, something dark happens: you start to think other people don't do "being a Christian" as well as you do. A frustration sets in that other people just "don't get it" like you do. You determine to obey with all of YOUR strength, and as YOU get better at it, YOU start to rely on You, and believe in....YOU. That's a lot of "yous," but that is my point. You actually drive yourself further from God (and other people) this way, when the whole point was to get closer to God.

If we have a close relationship with God, there is fire and passion in our heart for the reading, praying, and serving. We don't have to TRY to do those things, we WANT to do those things. When your heart catches fire with passion for Jesus, nothing is going to get in the way of reading HIS words, and talking to HIM, and serving people because HE told you to.

Now, I am evidence of the fact that a person can have no understanding of this concept and still find themselves growing increasingly close to God. God used a couple of times in my life to draw me close. They were both near- tragedies. The first one occurred when I was about 27. At this time of my life my marriage fell apart and my wife wanted to leave me at the same time we found out we were pregnant with my oldest son, Noah. The second happened when I was about 30. I had just started a business and went several years with an extreme lack of money. God used these circumstances in my life to show me, in ways I will never forget, that I really needed more of Him and His ways, and less of me and my ways, to survive. God uses all things for the good of those who love Him (Romans 8:28) and sometimes a little near-tragedy is exactly what we need to teach us how to give God more of our heart. However, Jesus told us exactly how to give Him ALL of our hearts, and His plan didn't include us having to wait for something really scary to happen.

A Roadmap to Wholeheartedness

Jesus' plan for wholeheartedness is laid out plainly in the Sermon on the Mount. Now, if you live in America, the Sermon on the Mount, when you really look at what it says, is going to sound like "Extreme Christianity." (That might make a good reality TV show, but most people don't like the sound of extreme Christianity.) What we have to remember is that Jesus wasn't saying the Sermon on the Mount was extreme, He was saying this lifestyle is the only relationship with Him there really is. You can read the whole Sermon on the Mount in Matthew Chapters 5, 6, and 7, but I want you to read the first part of the Sermon on the Mount, Matthew 5:1-11 now:

> *(Matthew 5:1-2)   One day as He saw the crowds gathering, Jesus went up on the mountainside and sat down. His disciples gathered around Him, and He began to teach them.*
>
> *5:3 "God blesses those who are poor and realize their need for Him, for the Kingdom of Heaven is theirs.*
>
> *5:4 God blesses those who mourn, for they will be comforted.*

5:5 God blesses those who are humble, for they will inherit the whole earth.

5:6 God blesses those who hunger and thirst for justice, for they will be satisfied.

5:7 God blesses those who are merciful, for they will be shown mercy.

5:8 God blesses those whose hearts are pure, for they will see God.

5:9 God blesses those who work for peace, for they will be called the children of God.

5:10 God blesses those who are persecuted for doing right, for the Kingdom of Heaven is theirs.

5:11 God blesses you when people mock you and persecute you and lie about you and say all sorts of evil things against you because you are My followers."

When you hear that list of blessed people, it probably doesn't line up with your "5 Favorite Ways to Spend The Weekend" list. When I first started reading this list, it didn't make a lot of sense. As I have learned to grow in wholeheartedness, and have heard other people teach about this, Jesus has begun to bring it into focus for me. I want to break it down a little bit so you can see what I have been seeing. You are really going to want to spend some time studying Matthew Chapters 5, 6, and 7. These verses are a recipe for giving every part of your life fully to God when you

take them all together. They are all part of the s
Jesus delivered on the mount.

Spiritual Poverty

Let's break down this passage a little, and you will start to see what I am talking about. We'll start with verse 3 *"God blesses those who are poor and realize their need for him..."* When you read that, you might be tempted to think Jesus was talking about money. He's not. He's not saying "if you are broke, heaven is yours, and if you are rich, look out." Jesus is saying we are blessed when we realize we are spiritually poor. That means, when you see what God says is available to you, and then realize you don't have it yet, and realize you need God to give it to you, you are blessed. Jesus is saying when this happens, you are on the right track to get more of the Kingdom. So what are some things that might be available to you that you don't have yet?

You should put together a list, either in your head or written down, of what you desire. You can start to create your list of things God has made available to you through reading the Bible, listening to others that know God and seeing the way they live, or from praying and having God reveal something He wants you to have. Here is the list I am currently praying to have more of (your list should change over time as you learn and grow):

- More hunger and thirst for being close to God (I always want more, no matter how much I get...I want to be growing more and more on fire for Him)
- To love reading the Bible
- To love spending time praying

- Fascination with who Jesus is
- To see God's glory, to actually see a vision of Jesus, and to see angels (people in the Bible describe seeing all these)
- Vision for my future (I want to know God's plans for me)
- Friendship with the Holy Spirit who lives inside of me
- To remain in Jesus (to talk to Him all day...like a running conversation with Him as I go through my day)
- Wisdom and insight into what God is telling me to do and how to do it
- To hear God more clearly
- To operate in signs and wonders (healing people by praying for them, prophetically speaking, an increase in my prayer language)

I realize I am spiritually poor in all of these things. I know much more is available to me, and I know God wants me to have more of them. Jesus says I am blessed just to realize more is available to me. The world would say I should be jealous of others that are strong in these areas. I might be tempted to think maybe God doesn't love me like He loves other people who have more of these things in their lives, but Jesus says I should <u>know I am blessed</u> because I realize there is more available to me! That is the exact opposite of the world's way.

Asking and Receiving
Look at verse 5:4 *"God blesses those who mourn..."* It would be tempting to think Jesus is saying you are blessed if

you are sad. It's funny how the world would want you to believe that a good Christian isn't too happy, shouldn't enjoy things too much, and should spend most of their time feeling kind of down! That is NOT being a good Christian. Jesus is responding to verse 3. He is saying "when you realize you are spiritually poor, and then it makes you mournful, you are blessed, because God is going to comfort you (give you more of the things you are mourning not having)!" Jesus is saying the mourning is actually the road to getting more. What do you do when you mourn? You cry out! *Jesus is saying, when you realize there is more of the Kingdom available to you and you don't have it, cry out to God for more, and He will give it to you!* If you will trust Jesus in this, your life will go into "hyper-drive" for God.

Jesus had so much to say about asking and receiving from God. I could go on for hours about this one topic. It makes me so excited because when I learned this principle it changed everything about my relationship with God. There is so much He wants to show you, so much He wants to tell you, so much He wants to do through you, but He makes you start the process. God won't force you into more of Him.

There is a HUGE misconception in the Church, especially in America, about reaching for more of God. I think it is because as modern Christians we make a big deal about not being able to earn salvation. That is true, we can't earn salvation. Salvation is a free gift from God, but it was actually very expensive. Jesus paid for it, not us. It is totally wrong to think because salvation is free to us, growing in your relationship with God doesn't require any thought or effort. It does. Now some people realize effort is required to grow in our relationship with God, and they direct their effort toward themselves. This is legalism. Legalism is directing your effort toward you, rather than understanding God's process for receiving more of the Kingdom. Jesus laid out that process clearly. In Mark 10:5 (and Luke 18:17) Jesus says something amazing. Check it out:

> *(Mark 10:15) I tell you the truth, anyone who doesn't receive the Kingdom of God like a child will never enter it.*"

"WILL NEVER ENTER IT?" That sounds serious. We need to pay attention to what Jesus is saying about getting more of the Kingdom like a child. I want you to think about when you were a little kid. I mean like when you were 3 or 4. If you wanted something when you were 3 or 4 years old, what would you do to get it? Did you know how much things cost when you were 3? Did you know how they were made or where to buy them? Did you know how much work your mom or dad had to do to get the money to buy what you wanted? No! You just saw something you wanted and you asked for it. If your mom or dad thought it was good for you, they would give it to you. Jesus is saying "if you want more of the Kingdom, you are going to have to humble yourself and just ask God for it. You can't earn it. Do you know how much the things of the Kingdom are worth? They are priceless! No amount of self effort is going to earn them for you."

Jesus is saying "reading your Bible more can't earn you a fiery relationship with God. Only asking the Father for it in My name will do it!" What is amazing is that when I started asking God for this, He started to give me a more fiery relationship with Him, and all I wanted to do was read more of my Bible! The difference is that I don't want to read my Bible TO get closer to God, I want to read it because I AM getting closer to God. Reading the Bible is what I WANT to do. I am not trying to earn anything from God. This is the difference between a religion and a relationship. Jesus is waiting to have a deep and real relationship with us. He's already chosen to go after more of us, but He patiently waits for us to choose to go after more of Him.

Look at what Jesus said about asking and receiving and how He says that it is just like a child asking and receiving:

> *(Luke 11:9-13) "And so I tell you, keep on asking, and you will receive what you ask for. Keep on seeking, and you will find. Keep on knocking, and the door will be opened to you.   For everyone who asks, receives. Everyone who seeks, finds. And to everyone who knocks, the door will be opened. "You fathers—if your children ask for bread, do you give them a stone? Or if they ask for a fish, do you give them a snake instead? Or if they ask for an egg, do you give them a scorpion? Of course not!   So if you sinful people know how to give good gifts to your children, how much more will your heavenly Father give the Holy Spirit to those who ask Him."*

Warning - God Tests Our Desire

Asking God for more is so simple anyone can do it, but so simple very few will actually do it with any consistent effort. For some reason, we trick ourselves into thinking it can't be this easy. And the truth is, it is not always easy to just keep asking. If you are going to start trying this out and asking God for more of the things you are spiritually poor in, you have to understand one very important principle: Jesus tests your desire for more of the Kingdom. Really! He wants to know how bad you really want it. He said this in several places when He talked about prayer. I want you to read one true story where you can see Jesus actually test someone's desire for more of the Kingdom (in this case healing). Check it out:

> *(Matthew 15:21-28) Then Jesus left Galilee and went north to the region of Tyre and Sidon. A Gentile woman who lived there came to Him, pleading, "Have mercy on me, O Lord, Son of David! For my daughter is possessed by a demon that torments her severely." But Jesus gave her no reply, not even a word. Then His disciples urged Him to send her away. "Tell her to go away," they said. "She is bothering us with all her begging."*

> *Then Jesus said to the woman, "I was sent only to help God's lost sheep—the people of Israel." But she came and worshiped Him, pleading again, "Lord, help me!"*

> *Jesus responded, "It isn't right to take food from the children and throw it to the dogs." She replied, "That's true, Lord, but even dogs are allowed to eat the scraps that fall beneath their masters' table."*

> *"Dear woman," Jesus said to her, "your faith is great. Your request is granted." And her daughter was instantly healed.*

This is an amazing passage, and I want to break it down a little bit. First, look at the woman's situation:

1. She is not Jewish, but she knows Jesus is the Messiah. That is why she called Him the Lord, Son of David.

2. She is asking for help for her little girl. Jesus said many times that He feels strongly about taking care of little kids.

3. The little girl is being attacked by a demon. Jesus came to take the world back from satan and demons.

Now look at Jesus' first response...Nada. He didn't even answer her! That does not sound like Jesus at all.   But look at what the woman does. She's keeps asking. The disciples said she begged for help even after Jesus ignored her. This is amazing!

Now look at what Jesus says next: *"I was sent only to help God's lost sheep—the people of Israel."* He told her she didn't qualify for help, but look at her response: she worshipped Him! Can you imagine Jesus ignoring you, then telling you he wasn't going to help you because you weren't the "right kind of person" and then, rather than give up praying, you worship Him instead!

Look at what happens next. Jesus says: *"It isn't right to take food from the children and throw it to the dogs."* The woman still does not give up. Jesus just insulted her and her daughter! This does not sound like Jesus at all. But look at what the woman says: *That's true, Lord, but even dogs are allowed to eat the scraps that fall beneath their masters' table."* The woman would not give up. She believed Jesus was the savior, that He had the ability to help her, and she knew His heart was for her. Even when it looked like He wouldn't give her what she needed, she pressed in.

IT IS SO IMPORTANT THAT WE GET THIS. This is the key to getting more of the Kingdom. We must refuse to give up or get upset when God doesn't answer our prayers for more immediately. We must keep pressing in with worship and praying for more.

Humility is Required

Let's get back to the Sermon on the Mount. We made it through the first two blessings including knowing we are poor and then asking (mourning) for more. Let's look at verse 5:

> *5:5 God blesses those who are humble, for they will inherit the whole earth.*

Humility is what you need after you've realized what you want more of, you've asked for more, and God has given it to you. You have to remain humble. Jesus knows when we follow this plan and humble ourselves to cry out for more, that God will meet our prayers with more of the Kingdom. Getting more of the Kingdom is powerful. You will feel differently about life. People will notice something different. When this happens, you really want to stay humble. It is easy to start to think you understand more than others, or that God is growing things in you that are uncommon. That might be true, but you need to remember that God is the source and not you. You didn't earn a fiery relationship with God, you just asked and received!

Let's take the next few verses as a group. These all sprout from the humility we learn to grow (ask for) in verse 5:

5:6-9 God blesses those who hunger and thirst for justice, for they will be satisfied. God blesses those who are merciful, for they will be shown mercy. God blesses those whose hearts are pure, for they will see God. God blesses those who work for peace, for they will be called the children of God.

As we begin to ask and receive more of the Kingdom, and ask for (and learn) humility, our hunger and our thirst for the things of God naturally increases. Jesus says when this happens we will be more and more satisfied in our lives with Him. The "switch will flip" in our understanding of what it means to give Him everything. Our lives will begin to look more like His, with our eyes focused on Him and the things of Him. Our lives stop looking so balanced and actually begin to be overtaken by a Kingdom mentality. This is the start of wholeheartedness.

Persecution Comes With The Territory

Mercy, pureness, and peace will be signs of our relationship with Him. We begin to understand what it might look like to live in a way where we want to be ruined for this world and only want more of Him and His ways. Our thoughts and dreams about the future start to regularly extend beyond the 70 or 80 years we might live on this earth and into our future in heaven. We start wanting to store treasure in heaven, and not here anymore. This is awesome, because we will live in heaven a LOT longer than we live here, but look at what comes next. It is a little hard to swallow:

5:10-11 God blesses those who are persecuted for doing right, for the Kingdom of Heaven is theirs. God

*blesses you when people mock you and persecute you
and lie about you and say all sorts of evil things against
you because you are My followers."*

This can be a big road block in our pursuit of Jesus.
What Jesus was saying was this: when you pursue this plan to
be a Christian, and you follow my instructions by examining
your life, realizing your lack, asking for more, and then
pursuing a life of asking for more in humility, people are going
to notice a huge change in you, and it is going to make them
very uncomfortable.

When people see you on fire for God, and having a
one-track mind for Jesus, it makes them very uncomfortable.
People don't like to feel like they have less than you. If they
would take Jesus' advice and know they are blessed, and
would ask Him for more, then they would be glad they
watched you become a fiery lover of God. People often don't
know this plan, and jealousy takes the place of asking for
more. Worse yet, the enemy comes along and lies to them,
telling them either you, or God, are judging their lack of
excitement for God. At this point people usually do one of a
few things:

- They might call you legalistic
- They might minimize your experience to make
  you feel like it is just you faking it
- They might make fun of you

Jesus says, when these things happen, don't give up.
Know you are blessed. Look at what He says in verse 12:

(Matthew 5:12) Be happy about it! Be very glad! For a great reward awaits you in heaven. And remember, the ancient prophets were persecuted in the same way.

Fuel for the Fire

In the rest of Matthew Chapters 5, 6 and 7, Jesus describes in more detail how to grow these qualities in our heart. These are actions we can take that will make the process of turning our lives over to Him faster. I want to just highlight a few. Entire books have been written on the Sermon on the Mount. This is something we will spend the rest of our lives studying. My goal is to start you off in the right direction. Look at Chapter 6 for just a minute. Look at the subject headings (if your Bible has them) in this Chapter. Now do the same thing in Chapter 7.

Jesus is describing some specific actions we can take to soften our heart to receive more of Him. I will generally list them:

- Charitable Giving in Secret (6:1-4)
- Fasting and Praying (6:5-18)
- Resisting Worry about Food, Clothing, Possessions and Focusing on Heavenly Rewards (6:19-34)
- Resisting Judging Others (7:1-6)
- Staying Steady in Asking for More (7:7-11)

When we practice doing these activities, it changes our "emotional chemistry." We don't earn more of God's favor or presence through doing these activities, but we do position our heart in a way that speeds up the process of receiving more of the Kingdom. I heard a Bible teacher explain it like this: when we decide to do these activities, it is like placing our hearts in front of a bonfire (picture God's fiery love for us). The fire will begin to soften and tenderize our heart to receive more from God, and more quickly. I want to talk about a couple of these activities briefly, because they are essential to follow Jesus in the way He directed us.

Charitable Giving in Secret (Matthew 6:1-4)

Jesus spent a lot of time in the Gospels talking about money. Money has a power over us. We forget that we can trust God to provide what we need, and we try to take care of it ourselves. It is so easy for us to put our trust in what we can see. I know you probably don't have a lot of money right now, but setting the right heart attitude when you have a little money will keep your heart steady as you get more. In fact, I want you to see what Jesus says about being faithful with a little bit:

> (Luke 16:9-11) Here's the lesson: Use your worldly resources to benefit others and make friends. Then, when your earthly possessions are gone, they will welcome you to an eternal home. "If you are faithful in little things, you will be faithful in large ones. But if you are dishonest in little things, you won't be honest with greater responsibilities.   And if you are untrustworthy about worldly wealth, who will trust you with the true riches of heaven?

Secrecy is another key here. Jesus made a point that those who give secretly will be rewarded, and those who don't, won't. You might think missing out on a reward means you won't be rewarded with more money later, that is part of what He is saying. However, I believe the lack of reward is really associated with this lifestyle of pressing in to God. He is saying, "if your heart isn't in the right mode when you give (if you give to be noticed, or you give to get more money) then your heart will not be positioned to receive the amazing rewards of the Kingdom lifestyle." This is the goal, to get the amazing riches of the Kingdom that will last forever, not the rusting and decaying riches of this life.

Prayer and Fasting (Matthew 6:5-18)

Prayer and fasting is essential for us to move forward in our pursuit of God. Jesus didn't say "if you pray or fast," he said "when you pray" and "when you fast" (Matthew 6:16). We need to continually ask God for a better prayer life. Fasting (giving something you enjoy up for a little while) speeds up everything. **If you are under 18, you should not fast from food.** There are a ton of ways to fast. You can fast whatever it is that you find most distracting from your reaching for more of the Kingdom. But when you fast, secrecy is key. Fasting something like Facebook is great, but telling everyone on Facebook that you are fasting Facebook completely changes it from being about drawing near to God, and instead it draws attention to you. There is no spiritual reward in drawing attention to yourself.

I think fasting is one of the most powerful, but also one of the most misunderstood, tools Jesus gave us to draw near to Him.   Satan will always try to "pull" your fasting into legalism. Our common sense tells us that if fasting is good, more and harder fasting must be better. I completely disagree. I believe weak fasting can be more powerful than harder fasting.   Weak fasting (intentionally giving up something in order to draw near to God, but not making it so dramatic that it is extremely uncomfortable) takes the emphasis off of what you are doing and places it on the rewards of simple obedience to what Jesus said to do.

I don't want to talk too much about this, because you *really* need to get direction directly from God, but I will tell you my own experience. When I started fasting, I would try to fast from food regularly from sundown to sundown (24 hours). This was tough for me to do, and it required making an issue of not eating dinner with my family on the night of the fast. It drew a lot of unnecessary attention to me, as my family ate without me. I felt like I was really honoring God in my "hard" fast, and I could see the spiritual effects for sure. However, after a while I got tired of making it such a big deal, and it was hard to plan for a whole day of not eating. Eventually, I switched to just skipping breakfast and lunch on my day of fasting. It is easy for me to keep this fast with no one realizing it. I have found out that I fast a lot more often doing it this way, and the breakthrough I am experiencing in growing closer to God is amazing. It has taken the emphasis off of "what I am doing for God" and placed it on "what I receive from God in simple obedience." I recommend you get your direction from Jesus on what to fast, how often to fast, and how long to fast. No matter what, fasting is essential.

Resisting Worry/Treasure and Rewards in Heaven (Matthew 6:19-34)

Jesus said many times to resist worry. Here, He focuses on worry about what you will wear or eat. Jesus is telling us to practice taking a "longer life view." We are almost completely absorbed with thinking about 70 or 80 short years on earth. The average American adult life literally revolves around enjoying our days to the fullest, saving for retirement, getting a more comfortable house, a better car, planning for the future. We have no way of knowing what the future holds for us, but often we will not help someone in need if we think it might negatively affect our plans for the future. In America, we are broken by our short sighted and material view of things. Worry about how much we have actually prevents us from going deeper in the amazing things of God and getting the spiritual rewards, both now and in heaven, of trusting God for what we need.

Jesus is giving us a huge warning. In America, our unbelievably comfortable life (in comparison to some other parts of the world) has messed up our view of reality. Ask anyone who has traveled beyond our borders and they will confirm this. Jesus said the choices you make in the extremely short 70 or 80 years in this life will affect the quality of your life FOREVER. Jesus spent a lot of time talking about treasure in heaven (Matthew 6:19-21, for example) and rewards in heaven. There are so many verses about rewards in heaven, I could not even come close to listing them all. A great quick study is to read Revelation Chapters 2 and 3 and look at the rewards for those who "overcome." There are rewards in heaven based on how we live our lives here and how well we love Jesus. Those rewards are enjoyed in heaven for eternity.

You might think: I am not into Jesus for the rewards, I don't need them. This is a completely un-Biblical attitude. Jesus taught about the rewards in heaven, and how they are based on our choices in this life. To think the rewards are shallow or unnecessary is to disagree with the message Jesus delivered. He told us about the rewards to motivate us to be wholehearted in our love for Him...to chase after Him with everything. You want to study and look forward to the rewards! You will be with Jesus forever.

Imagine not loving Him with everything you have in this short life, and then being with Him forever in heaven. You will wish you had made some different choices on earth after 1 or 2 million years of being with Him and knowing you didn't give your all when you could have. I am not trying to lay guilt on you for the choices you have made in the past, but now that you know, decide to love Him well. He loved you with literally everything (even dying for you), and still does. If you will take Him seriously on this point now, when you are face to face with Him, you can celebrate more of your love for Him and the adventures you undertook for Him in your short life on earth.

Resisting Judging Others and Continuing to Ask for More (Matthew 7:1-6)

There is a temptation, as people resist you for being wholehearted, to judge what other people do. This is particularly tempting when dealing with other people who are following Jesus. Jesus is saying that if you will keep your focus on what God is doing in your life, it will help you resist the temptation to judge others. Judging others has the opposite effect of softening our hearts. It quickly hardens our hearts and makes good soil for pride and anger to grow. This is a strategy of satan to pull you away from your pursuit of God.

Satan wants you to pursue yourself, or to compare yourself to others. You have to know that Jesus warns us about judging others because He knows we will do it. The enemy will try to heap guilt on you when you realize you have sinned in this way. Don't fall for this double-whammy. When you catch yourself in judgment, simply admit it to God, agree with Him that it is sin, ask His forgiveness in Jesus' name, and get back to asking Him for more of the Kingdom. Learn from

David's story (you can find it in 1 Samuel and 2 Samuel), when you mess up, agreeing with God fully restores you. Waste no time on guilt.

Following the Sermon on the Mount, examining our lives for spiritual poverty, asking for more (mourning our lack), asking for humility, and then accelerating everything with a steady prayer life, fasting, and giving, is the roadmap for following Jesus, as He defined it. This lifestyle is what Jesus said it means to be one of His followers. This isn't radical Christianity, this is the only Christianity there is.

Wholeheartedness is the key to changing the geographic area you live in. Remember how we talked about Abraham's conversation with the Lord before He destroyed Sodom. If even 10 people would have been found in the city who were in a right relationship with God, the whole city would have been spared. Right now, all around you, God is sending this message out to His people. He is sending it to you. For so long people in America have bought into a self-help version of following Jesus, a faith almost void of any real hunger or thirst for more of Jesus. A lot of us get "saved" and then spend years getting comfortable with our new security. We try to find the line of how much of the world we can have and still have Jesus. It is so common, and we see it all around us at Church, we think this is normal Christianity. This is not normal. This is sickly Christianity.

Think about your own body. If you go very long without hunger or thirst, you would be considered sick, and would be making your way to the doctor's office. Many people in the Church have a faith that is in the ICU, and they don't even know it. They judge the intensity of their walk with God by comparing it to others around them. ***Jesus requires everything.*** Following Jesus is not an add-on accessory to a good life, it's a radical (to the world) redefining of what life is. Following Jesus requires dying to ourselves and focusing totally on Him. Check out what Jesus said:

> *(Matthew 16:24-27) Then Jesus said to His disciples, "If any of you wants to be My follower, you must turn from your selfish ways, take up your cross, and follow Me. If you try to hang on to your life, you will lose it. But if you give up your life for My sake, you will save it. And what do you benefit if you gain the whole world but lose your own soul? Is anything worth more than your soul? For the Son of Man will come with His angels in the glory of His Father and will judge all people according to their deeds.*

When you start asking God for more, the way Jesus described in the Sermon on the Mount, you will find out that losing your life for Jesus' sake is a really good deal! It sounds like you are going to be giving up everything "fun" in life. This is what I thought. For years I resisted being wholehearted. I told myself I needed balance. I didn't want to be one of those weird people always talking about Jesus. When I started to ask God for more of the Kingdom, and He started to give it to me, my interest in having a balanced life just naturally began to fade away. I started to find God more fascinating than the stuff I was trying to hold onto.

Asking God for more, the way Jesus described it in the Sermon on the Mount, actually dramatically changed what I want to fill my life with. It changed what I see as appealing and interesting. Reaching for God makes me hungrier for things that draw me closer to Jesus. God has miraculously reorganized my priorities in life. If you will let Him, God will reorganize your life, too. When this happens, it won't be something that is driven by your strength, it will be driven by receiving God's love for you.

A Light To the World

When we begin trying to live the Sermon on the Mount, we will radically change our understanding of how God feels about us. This starts a cycle of growth that changes everything about our lives. It sets our hearts on fire for the life Jesus described. A life that is dead to self and alive only in Jesus. But this is the deal: Jesus wants us to radically change where we live. He wants us to create geographic islands of mercy as He prepares to execute His plans to judge everything that gets in the way of His love. The fate of your city literally lies in your willingness to go after God with your whole heart. It isn't enough to just quietly chase this life. Jesus told us to let others "see" what we are doing. Check it out:

> (Matthew 5:14-16) "You are the light of the world—
> like a city on a hilltop that cannot be hidden. No one
> lights a lamp and then puts it under a basket. Instead,
> a lamp is placed on a stand, where it gives light to
> everyone in the house. In the same way, let your good
> deeds shine out for all to see, so that everyone will
> praise your heavenly Father.

Jesus wants as many people to know Him as possible. It is not His will that anyone would be separated from Him for eternity. Jesus doesn't want anyone to go to Hell. It is our job to live the way He told us to, and then as people around us notice the difference in our lives, to tell them about the treasure we have found in living 100% for Jesus.

Wholeheartedness has a dramatic effect on how people see you. For some, it is absolutely contagious, for others, it is absolutely irritating. If you will keep your gaze on God, and resist judging others, you will find that you are changing lives all around you. You will be creating a geographic area of blessing that will be a safe haven as Jesus moves forward in His plan to judge everything that gets in the way of His love. The land of Goshen, that geographic place of protection from judgment, could be right under your feet! We have a responsibility to Jesus, not to mention those we know and love, to work at making our city a place of blessing and protection. Wholehearted love for God is how we get back on the Ancient Highway. This is what it means to be salt and light!

Jesus Wants to What?! - 4

Jesus wants to marry you. If you are a guy, you just cringed. If you are a girl, maybe you just got an idea of a candle-lit dinner. For me, this is one of the hardest ideas in the Bible to wrap my head around. The Bible says it over and over. John the Baptist said it. Jesus' good friend John said it in the Book of Revelation. Even the prophets of old, including Isaiah, Jeremiah, and Hosea knew this was God's heart for His people. When we think of marriage we think joint checking accounts and making babies, but when God talks about marriage He is describing a sacred agreement that changes our position in a family. He wants us to "marry-up" into His royal family!

Jeremiah prophesied that near the end of the age, messengers would be sent out into the world to teach people how God felt about them. I believe some of you reading this book are the very messengers Jeremiah prophesied about. Check it out:

> *(Jeremiah 3:15) And I will give you shepherds after My own heart, who will guide you with knowledge and understanding.*

The phrase "after My own heart" is significant. This was the phrase God used to describe David, the man after His own heart. David, one of the toughest and greatest warriors of all time, was also one of the most intense "God-lovers" of all time. David filled the Psalms with songs about gazing upon God's beauty, delighting in His perfection, experiencing His everlasting forgiveness, and compassion, and protection. David knew God wanted him to experience the privilege of knowing God's heart; being close to God like an actual son.

What Does God Mean by Marriage?

You see, the message of people being married to Jesus is not about putting on a wedding dress, holding some flowers, and worshipping God. It isn't about dancing with Jesus through fields, or holding hands with Him while walking down streets of gold. The message of being the Bride of Christ is about the unique privilege reserved for people who belong to the Lord. It is the privilege of being a "partner" with Jesus. **It is about your high position in the royal family of Jesus, God the Father, and the Holy Spirit.** This privilege is for boys and girls, men and women. Just like marriage on earth, the Bible is describing a legal family position where we enjoy the closest relationship with God there is.   A position of intense confidence in God's love for us and freedom to love Him back. This is a family position that only humans saved by Jesus can experience.

The apostle Paul said that this special relationship we have with God, and His plans for us because of it, are beyond our wildest imagination. Look at what Paul told the Church in Corinth:

> *(1 Corinthians 2:7-13) No, the wisdom we speak of is the mystery of God—His plan that was previously hidden, even though He made it for our ultimate glory before the world began. But the rulers of this world have not understood it; if they had, they would not have crucified our glorious Lord.   That is what the Scriptures mean when they say, "No eye has seen, no*

ear has heard, and no mind has imagined what God has prepared for those who love Him." But it was to us that God revealed these things by His Spirit. For His Spirit searches out everything and shows us God's deep secrets. No one can know a person's thoughts except that person's own spirit, and no one can know God's thoughts except God's own Spirit. And we have received God's Spirit (not the world's spirit), so we can know the wonderful things God has freely given us.

Paul was saying that God's plan for people was designed for our glory. Then he goes on to describe how our glory was connected to Jesus, our glorious Lord, dying on a cross. He said "no mind has imagined" the wonderful things God has prepared for those who love Him. Paul was describing the desire of God to "partner" his people to our glorious Lord, Jesus...to bring them into His royal family.

I'm a guy. When I first heard that Jesus wants me to marry me, it made me feel pretty weird. I got hung up on the world's ideas about marriage. The bridal relationship God is describing isn't a boy and girl thing. It isn't about a physical relationship but a spiritual and legal relationship between two people that God calls marriage throughout the Bible. God didn't get the idea for marriage from us, we got it from Him. We need to remember that our ideas about marriage may not be quite right. Our ideas are often shaped by the world we live in.

Have you noticed how the whole idea of marriage is very controversial? You hear about it in the news all the time. Divorce, broken families, affairs, gay marriage...these are in the headlines daily. Numerous movies and TV shows subtly try to tell us how to think about marriage. Marriage, and the idea of what a marriage is, has been under attack for a long time. Because of this, we have a lot of weird ideas about what marriage is, or isn't. It is important that we know exactly what God means by marriage, and why He chose marriage as the metaphor for our relationship with Jesus.

Remember how Jeremiah said in the last days God would raise up messengers after His own heart? Understanding we (the Church) are Jesus' bride is going to become more and more important as Jesus' plan to remove evil from the planet unfolds. When we begin to understand Jesus as a groom, we will begin to understand more fully who we are, and what our role with Jesus is as He takes His rightful place as king and ruler over all. When a husband becomes king, the wife has it made!

So what does God intend marriage to be? The Bible is full of information about marriage.   When asked about marriage and divorce, Jesus described what happens when a man and woman get married. This is what Jesus said:

> *(Mark 10:8-9) and the two are united into one.' Since they are no longer two but one, let no one split apart what God has joined together."*

Jesus was saying that marriage legally makes two people connected as if they are one. They are still two distinct people, but by marriage, the law sees them as one person, linked so closely, they are inseparable. In our world, marriage usually doesn't seem this permanent. Divorce happens so often, we start to think of marriage as less than what God desired. When depictions of married people are portrayed on TV or in movies, often it doesn't appear that the two married people are acting like one. Usually, it is exactly the opposite.

The media portrays married people at odds with each other. Often, TV shows and movies show a "dumb" husband being harassed by an overpowering wife, or a husband that is trying to hide something from his wife, or vice versa.   Usually marriage as we see it on TV, in books, and in movies doesn't convey the strong connection God intended for a husband and a wife to have with each other.

The enemy doesn't want you to understand what real marriage is supposed to look like, or how strong a marriage is supposed to be. Marriage is a sacred partnership. The most special relationship a person can have with another person. God wants to use a right idea of marriage to explain how He feels about us. Satan is afraid that if you find out how God feels about you, you will be much more determined to turn your whole life over to Him. *God is completely committed to you. When you realize this, you will desire to be completely committed to Him.*

Understanding marriage is the key to understanding what your future with Jesus is all about. Look at how God described marriage through the apostle Paul:

> *(Ephesians 5:21-32)   And further, submit to one another out of reverence for Christ.   For wives, this means submit to your husbands as to the Lord. For a husband is the head of His wife as Christ is the head of the Church. He is the Savior of His body, the Church. As the Church submits to Christ, so you wives should submit to your husbands in everything.*
>
> *For husbands, this means love your wives, just as Christ loved the Church. He gave up His life for her to make her holy and clean, washed by the cleansing of God's*

word. He did this to present her to Himself as a glorious Church without a spot or wrinkle or any other blemish. Instead, she will be holy and without fault.   In the same way, husbands ought to love their wives as they love their own bodies. For a man who loves his wife actually shows love for himself.

No one hates his own body but feeds and cares for it, just as Christ cares for the Church.   And we are members of his body.   As the Scriptures say, "A man leaves his father and mother and is joined to his wife, and the two are united into one."   This is a great mystery, but it is an illustration of the way Christ and the Church are one.

This was always God's intent for marriage: a relationship where a husband loved and served his wife, and the wife respected and trusted the husband for leadership and protection. In our selfish world, neither of those roles sound very appealing, but God knew this sort of relationship was so powerful nothing could separate two people who decided to enter into it willingly. Because of the way our world looks at marriage, we get caught up in a "what is in it for me?" attitude, this messes up our entire view of what God meant marriage to be.

In our world, the emphasis in marriage is what a person gets out of it, even sometimes for people in the Church. In our selfishness, we easily think of marriage in terms of sex, stability, money, and kids. For a lot of people, if marriage "makes sense" for them, they will commit to it, if it doesn't, they want to quit. This is the opposite of how the Bible describes marriage. Maybe you aren't married yet, but you know that if you hang out with someone who is only interested in themselves, they aren't enjoyable to be around. Add the pressure of responsibility which comes with adult life, and you get a full-on tragedy-in-the-making.   Many married couples don't get that marriage is about loving and serving, not getting and taking.

God Wants You to Be With Him Where He Is

Rather than what we are going to get out of marriage, God wanted people to consider what they would put into marriage. God wants you to know how much Jesus wants to put into our marriage partnership with Him. As crazy as it might seem to us, Jesus' intention has always been that we would enjoy a relationship with God just like the one He has. He paid for it with His life. Jesus was willing to come down from heaven, and forever live in the limitations of being a man, just so we could share His position with God and all of the power, honor, and glory that goes with it. Look at the conversation God (Jesus) had with God (the Father) just before He sacrificed Himself for us on the cross:

> *(John 17:20-26)   "I am praying not only for these disciples but also for all who will ever believe in Me through their message. I pray that they will all be one, just as You and I are one—as You are in Me, Father, and I am in You. And may they be in Us so that the world will believe You sent Me. "I have given them the glory You gave Me, so they may be one as We are one. I am in them and You are in Me. May they experience such perfect unity that the world will know that You sent Me and that You love them as much as You love Me. Father, I want these whom You have given Me to*

be with Me where I am. Then they can see all the glory You gave Me because You loved Me even before the world began! "O righteous Father, the world doesn't know You, but I do; and these disciples know You sent Me. I have revealed You to them, and I will continue to do so. Then Your love for Me will be in them, and I will be in them."

I could read this conversation between God Jesus and God the Father over and over. It never gets old for me. When you lock into what Jesus is saying, I think you will feel the same way. Look at what He says about you: that you would be <u>one with Him</u>; that He has <u>given you His glory</u>; That we (the Church) would be <u>one like Jesus and God are one</u>, and that we would then be <u>one with God the Father, Jesus, and the Holy Spirit</u>. This passage is so packed with amazing goodness you could spend years meditating on it and never scratch the surface of how big Jesus' statement is for humans. Jesus said God the Father loves us as much as He loves Jesus! The intensity of God's love for us is almost too good to be true, but it IS true.

Jesus said He will make us so close to Him that when the world looks at us, they will actually see Him. In John 14:7, Jesus said if we have seen Him and how He feels about things, then we have seen the Father and how He feels about things. The Father and Jesus' plan is that someday when the world sees us, they will know they have seen God! This is part of what it means to be married to Jesus. We can be so close to Him that we know how He feels about things, that we share in His glory, His honor, His power, and His position as King over all.

God wants us to understand marriage because this relationship is the foundational relationship He always desired for us to have with Him. Think about when He made Adam and Eve. He gave them dominion over the earth in partnership with Him. God has always wanted a family in us. Nothing else created gets to experience this partnership. Animals don't get to be God's family. Not even the angels get this kind of relationship with God (Hebrews 1:13-14; Hebrews 2:16). Only redeemed humans get to be "in the family." This is what our marriage to Jesus is all about. God's mysterious plan for us is that we would actually be so united to Him through Jesus, that we would be His sons, sharing everything Jesus owns, ruling with Jesus as King of Kings, submitting to Jesus for direction, and playing our role as His closest companion.

The great men of God understood this was the relationship God desired for us. Jesus said that John the Baptist was the greatest man ever born (Matthew 11:11). Listen to what John the Baptist said about himself:

(John 3:28-29) You yourselves know how plainly I told you, 'I am not the Messiah. I am only here to prepare the way for Him.' It is the bridegroom who marries the bride, and the best man is simply glad to stand with him and hear his vows. Therefore, I am filled with joy at His success.

We Have a High Position In God's Family

John the Baptist knew Jesus was coming to make the way for us to be back in God's family. We must find out for ourselves what this means. I am trying to point you in the right direction, but you will want to study this idea in the Bible for the rest of your life. The "mysterious plan" God has for us to be one with His Son, Jesus, has huge implications for you now, and in the future, forever and ever. You will want to begin asking God the Holy Spirit to reveal more of what being God's son means.

An understanding of this marriage relationship is important for the generation that witnesses Jesus coming as King. The Book of Revelation refers to the Church as Jesus' bride more than any other book in the Bible. Jeremiah Chapter 3, where God promises to give the world messengers after His own heart, comes just before Chapter 4, where God reveals through Jeremiah details about the end of the age, when Jesus' battle plan unfolds. God wants us to be confident that we are in His family, because He knows it will strengthen us for what is about to come over the whole world, the Great Tribulation. Without knowing we are actually in a marriage partnership to the one who is allowing the judgments to be released, the Great Tribulation would be the great terror. But He has made known this wonderful truth, that our beloved, our groom, is the one driving the events of Revelation, to give us confidence and security to be in the world to proclaim His great love as the terrified world gropes for answers!

Not only does God want us to understand we are in a marriage relationship with Jesus, He wants us to draw the next logical conclusion. When a husband and wife are married, the husband's parents become the wife's parents, too. When we think about our position this way, we realize through Jesus we become actual sons of God the Father! To be a son of the Living God is an amazing privilege. We can easily picture Jesus as God's son. He was born in a miraculous way and performed all sorts of miracles to prove He was God's son. But God wants us to be confident that because of our marriage to Jesus, we have become His sons, too (Hebrews 2:11)!

We might not realize how great it is to be a son of God. Many of the human fathers around us might not make us want to be sons or daughters of another father. The media plays such a strong role in shaping how this generation thinks about fathers, marriage, and family. The negative images of dads are overwhelming. Sitcoms and dramas have drastically changed how we see the concept of family. It is no coincidence that God uses the metaphors of marriage and fatherhood to explain who we are, and these are the very institutions under attack in our world. Our respect for, and love of, fathers has been incredibly damaged. We have to know God is a perfect father, wholly different than the idea a lot of us have of our earthly dad, if we even know him.

There are a few things about God our father we need to know. We want to spend time talking to God about these ideas. We want to ask the Holy Spirit to take us deeper in these truths. The more we understand God as our real Father, the more confident we will be in our conversations with Him. He REALLY thinks of you as His son. Just like both men and women are the Bride of Jesus, both men and women are also Sons of God. A relationship with God goes beyond gender. He wants us to understand our family position, not the roles guys and girls have in our earthly families. God the Father is this kind of Dad:

1.   **God is compassionate and is tender with us, even in our weakness.** I am an earthly dad, and I mess that job up sometimes. I get impatient. Sometimes I lash out when I am irritated. God is so unlike me. He isn't just tolerating you. A lot of times we feel like God is still holding a

grudge about the last time we messed up. When you come before Him to talk to Him in prayer, He doesn't think "oh great, it's you again!" He is just the opposite. He **delights** in hearing you. God knows that we are going to make mistakes. He knows we are going to mess up. He wants us to run **to** Him when we make a mistake, not run **from** Him.

We might doubt our ability to keep being good, but God knows whether or not we really want to do the right thing. There is a difference between intentional disobedience and immaturity. If we intentionally disobey God, He is not pleased. God is grieved when we rebel against Him, and sometimes we do that. We need to repent when we disobey God. But we also need to realize that often we don't intentionally rebel against Him. Have you ever made a mistake and as soon as you sinned, wished you hadn't? You say "God, I am sorry. I don't want to be that way. I don't want to do that again. Please help me!" This isn't rebellion, this is immaturity.

Often, especially when we are young, our <u>desire</u> to do good is stronger than our <u>ability</u> to resist sin. This is immature faith, not rebellion. God knows the difference, and He is so compassionate. He enjoys us *while* we are maturing. He isn't waiting for us to get it all right before He pours His love out on us. God knows weak love is still sincere; it's still real love. He loves our *sincere desire* to obey and love Him. Intentions matter with God. He doesn't want you to wait until you are perfect to enjoy His company. He wants you to experience His love right now.

Don't put yourself on probation when you mess up. To keep your relationship with God bright, deal with your mistakes right away. Run to Him. Just agree with Him that what you did was sin, declare war on it, and ask Him for help.

This is called repentance. When we repent, God is faithful to forgive us, completely, every time (1 John 1:9). We have to know God is a compassionate and tender father. Look at what Jesus said when He told the story of the prodigal son to describe to us how God our Father thinks of us:

> *(Luke 15:17-24) "When he finally came to his senses, he said to himself, 'At home even the hired servants have food enough to spare, and here I am dying of hunger! I will go home to my father and say, "Father, I have sinned against both heaven and you, and I am no longer worthy of being called your son. Please take me on as a hired servant."'*

> *"So he returned home to his father. And while he was still a long way off, his father saw him coming. Filled with love and compassion, he ran to his son, embraced him, and kissed him.   His son said to him, 'Father, I have sinned against both heaven and you, and I am no longer worthy of being called your son.' "But his father said to the servants, 'Quick! Bring the finest robe in the house and put it on him. Get a ring for his finger and sandals for his feet. And kill the calf we have been fattening. We must celebrate with a feast, for this son of mine was dead and has now returned to life. He was lost, but now he is found.' So the party began.*

Jesus used this parable to show us God's heart when we repent of our mistakes. When the son was still way off, just having decided to repent, the father jumped up and ran to him, threw his arms around his son, and kissed him. The son was right back in his rightful position as son of a great man.

The father didn't put the son on probation to see if he was really going to shape up. He threw the finest robe on his son and threw a party. This is how God wants to treat you. When we put ourselves on probation, and think God is just waiting to see if we will mess up again, we are totally missing the relationship God wants us to experience.

2. **God has a happy heart!** We have to first realize that God is compassionate and is tender with us, even in our weakness. Once we believe God is tender, we can jump into an even greater reality: God is mostly happy! So many times we think wrongly about God. We think He is mostly mad at us for messing up, or we think He is mostly disappointed with us because we blew it again. This couldn't be further from the truth. God is mostly happy. He was happy when He created people and called us "very good." Jesus was so happy as He ministered with His disciples He was accused of being a partier! (Luke 7:34). Listen to how David described God and how He feels about His children:

> *(Psalms 145:8) The LORD is merciful and compassionate, slow to get angry and filled with unfailing love. The LORD is good to everyone. He showers compassion on all His creation. All of Your works will thank You, LORD, and Your faithful followers will praise You. They will speak of the glory of Your kingdom; they will give examples of Your power. They will tell about Your mighty deeds and about the majesty and glory of Your reign. For Your kingdom is an everlasting kingdom. You rule throughout all generations. The LORD always keeps His promises; He is gracious in all He does. The LORD helps the fallen*

and lifts those bent beneath their loads.   The eyes of all look to You in hope; You give them their food as they need it.   When You open your hand, You satisfy the hunger and thirst of every living thing.   The LORD is righteous in everything He does; He is filled with kindness.

Being a child of the glad-hearted, kind, providing, and loving God is an awesome privilege. We want to spend hours and days meditating on how God thinks of us. Ask the Holy Spirit to take you deeper into this truth!

3.   **God has fiery desire to be with you and for you to know Him.** This is one of the most powerful truths in the Bible. The Song of Solomon is a parable about God's fiery desire for us. Understanding what this means is vital. When we see that God has fiery desire for us, those same feelings are reproduced in our heart. My favorite Bible teacher calls this "beholding and becoming." When we see and believe how God feels about us, we become people that feel the same way about God.

We feel like we are just one of billions of people God has to be responsible for. We see ourselves in a great sea of people. We would not admit it, but sometimes we imagine God to be like a movie star and we have to compete with a ton of other people hoping to shake His hand or get His autograph. This is the opposite of the truth. We have His full attention. You are God's favorite you. You are the only you He has ever made, and only you can love Him the way He designed you to love Him. No one else ever has had the ability to give God attention like you can. When God thinks of you,

His heart beats faster. The Bible says that one glance from you towards Him "captures His heart" (Song of Solomon 4:9).

God wants to be in a fiery relationship with you. A relationship filled with intensity and excitement, where you realize how special you are to Him; that you are His favorite. He has plans for you only you can carry out. He has a future planned for you that the Bible says you would hope for (Jeremiah 29:11). His love for you is so strong even death cannot hold it back. Check out my favorite verse from the Song of Songs:

> *(Song of Solomon 8:6) Place me like a seal over your heart, like a seal on your arm. For love is as strong as death, its jealousy as enduring as the grave. Love flashes like fire, the brightest kind of flame.*

Ask God to place himself like a seal over your heart. Ask Him to help you close your heart to all other loves but His. Once you get your sense of being loved directly from God, you will love others and receive love from them in a right way. He has already placed you like a seal over His heart. Jesus has already proven that His love for you is stronger than death!

The Confidence of the Bride Is Essential

The Bible describes the time that is about to come upon the earth in great detail. Jesus wants partners in His plan to drive evil off of the earth. We have an amazing role to play as Jesus' partners both at the end of this evil age, and in the age to come. Jesus, our partner, our groom, our best friend, is coming to rule over everything as king! He described in the Bible how His best friends get to rule and reign with Him! This describes you! We need to spend time asking the

Holy Spirit to help us imagine all this means, who we are, and how we can tell others about our privilege of being Jesus' partners. The trouble that is beginning to appear on planet earth has a lot of people beginning to wonder what life is really about. The trouble is going to get worse. The Bible is clear about this. But the Bible is also clear about Jesus' followers beginning to understand what it means to be married to the king, to be in the royal family. For a large portion of the modern Church, this is a whole new way of understanding what following Jesus is all about.

Confidence in who we are is essential if we want to be strong in the face of trouble. Jesus promised that if we stood for Him, we would face trouble (John 15:20). We have to know that Jesus is worth it. As we find out more about God's desire for us to be partners with Jesus, and we become confident we are the very sons of God, our strength to withstand trouble increases.

A lot of us want to be good workers for God. Sometimes I want to think of myself as a good soldier in God's army. Do you ever think of yourself this way? Wanting to work for God or to fight for Him is good, but we have to know the truth: God isn't interested in you just being a worker for Him. God doesn't want you to just be a soldier. A worker works for His pay, and a soldier fights because of their orders. Jesus wants you to be married to Him, He wants you to be part of the royal family.

When you are a close member of the family, you don't work for pay. When you really love someone, you serve them out of an overflowing love. When you are fighting for your family, you don't fight because it is your duty, you fiercely fight for family out of instinctive love. No one fights or works for the cause of their beloved like a family. Jesus feels this way about us. He proved it when He became a man to save us. He honored His marriage vows when He was beaten for our sins and hung on a cross for our mistakes. Even though He was and always will be God, He chose, because of love, to live in the limitations of being a man, and to take the punishment you deserved, because of how He feels about you. You are the apple of His eye, and when you start to understand this, you begin to know what it means to be married to Him, to be in His royal family. This realization will cause us to be bold for Him and confident that He will never leave us or forsake us as a time of trouble like no other engulfs the earth.

Think About Heaven! - 5

Not only is it important to know who we are, we must know where we are going if we want to be excited and steady as darkness increases. Try this: wherever you are at right now, look down. Imagine the start of a line right in front of you. Now, look to your right. Imagine the line that starts in front of you extends to the right as far as you can see. Is there a wall there? Imagine the line goes right through the wall and extends to your right...forever...and ever...and ever. Imagine it extends through the atmosphere, through the solar system, through the galaxies. It never ends. Ever. Now, imagine this line is a timeline. This timeline represents your life. If this line represents your life, think about how much of the line would represent the first 70 or 80 years of your life. Would it be an inch? How about a half of an inch? In the face of eternity, 70 years wouldn't be any more than the pin-point at the very start of your line.

Thinking about eternity gives me a headache sometimes. Imagining something as vast as eternity is hard. Thinking about heaven can be difficult too. Most of us know so little about what heaven is going to be like. When you think of heaven, what comes to your mind?

- Living on a cloud?
- Playing a harp?
- Worshipping God all the time?
- Angels?
- Seeing people who died before us?

The Bible Says to Think About Heaven

Do you think about heaven a little, or a lot? If you are like most people, you probably think about what it might be like a little, but then it is hard to understand or picture, so you don't think about it for very long. When we can't picture or imagine something, it is hard to get very excited about it. Getting excited about our future is exactly why Jesus really wants us to know about heaven. He wants us to be excited about where we will live forever.

If you are like most people, your plans and dreams center on what will happen in the next 10 years. Maybe, if you are really a long-range thinker, you imagine life all the way until you are "old." If your dreams are limited to this life, this age, where you have an aging body in a fallen world, then your decisions will reflect that. If you are thinking of the next 30 to 70 years, and then everything is unknown beyond that, then it would only be logical to plan the best choices to help you navigate the next 30 to 70 years. In the Bible, Jesus basically said "don't do that!"

Jesus wants your life vision to extend a long way past the next 70 years. He wants you to start to dream about your life in 100 years. Then He wants you to picture your life in 500 years, then a million, then a billion years from now. You are going to live forever. Jesus knows that your choices here will reflect how you picture yourself in the future. If you are living only for today, your choices will reflect that. Check out what the apostle Paul said to the Church in Colossae:

(Colossians 3:1-2) You have been raised to life with Christ, so set your hearts on the things that are in heaven, where Christ sits on his throne at the right side

of God. Keep your minds fixed on things there, not on things here on earth.

Jesus knows that if we think about heaven, and what it might be like, it will be easier for us to make decisions on earth that bring us closer to Him. God's desire is for us to be with Him! When we realize that this life on this earth is just a very short beginning to our eternity with God, we will choose to spend more time doing the things Jesus says will draw us closer to Him. The decisions we make on earth will look a lot different as our gaze extends beyond the earth we now know. The impact of our decisions on earth, in the short 70 or 80 years that mark the beginning of our life, actually determine how we will live for eternity. Look at what Jesus said to His disciples:

(Matthew 6:19-21) "Don't store up treasures here on earth, where moths eat them and rust destroys them, and where thieves break in and steal. Store your treasures in heaven, where moths and rust cannot destroy, and thieves do not break in and steal. Wherever your treasure is, there the desires of your heart will also be.

A Right View of Heaven Changes How We Live Now
What Jesus was saying here is important. Very few people think about saving up treasure in heaven. We don't want our idea of what is "fair" to blur the truth about heaven. It is so common for people to think that in heaven everyone wears the same thing, lives in the same place, and does the same thing. "Communist utopia" is the idea in many people's minds when they think of heaven. That is not what Jesus

described at all! Jesus said our wealth in heaven is linked to the choices we make in this life. In the passage we just read, Jesus was telling His disciples they could *actually* store treasure in heaven. This wasn't a metaphor! He was literally talking about earthly wealth and how our choices with it will determine part of the quality of our heavenly existence. He was basically saying "you people are tempted to store up things to make life comfortable here, but it won't last. You will be much happier if you store up things in heaven to make your life comfortable there. You'll be there forever, and your treasure will last there."

Jesus taught often about rewards in heaven. Jesus doesn't hand out rewards like the 3rd grade soccer team, where everyone gets the same trophy for participating. Jesus said that we would be rewarded for the choices we make here. Look at what He said about His return:

> *(Revelation 22:12) "Look, I am coming soon, bringing My reward with Me to repay all people according to their deeds.*

Rewards are mentioned 35 times in the New Testament, in addition to over 20 specific rewards listed in Chapters 2 and 3 of the Book of Revelation for those who "overcome" in specific ways in the last days. In the Sermon on the Mount, Jesus mentions specific rewards for things like enduring persecution from those who oppose us (Matthew 5:12), loving our enemies (Matthew 5:46), giving in secret (Matthew 6:4), praying privately (Matthew 6:6), and fasting privately (Matthew 6:16). Rewards are also mentioned by Jesus and the apostles for being ready when Jesus returns, showing kindness to those who cannot pay you back, investing what God has given you in the Kingdom, doing good deeds, and showing kindness to other believers. The list goes on and on. How you choose to spend your time and your money, and what you let your heart focus on while you are on earth, will significantly affect your rewards, or your quality of life, in heaven.

God says we should set our eyes on heaven, and not on things here because He *really* wants to reward us. He wants us to be able to enjoy the fact that we loved Jesus well on earth before He returns. We will be with Jesus for eternity, and we will wish we had served Him with all of our heart when we see Him face to face. The rewards, when we understand them, make us want to live wholeheartedly for Jesus.

You might think you aren't into Jesus for the rewards. It might seem better, or more holy, to not care about rewards, but that disagrees with what Jesus taught. Jesus taught about heavenly rewards more than anyone else! We want to listen to Jesus and not our own ideas of what is right or holy.

Thinking about heaven helps us make choices that honor God and result in rewards. So, what is there to know about heaven in the Bible? The Bible actually says a lot about heaven. The world also says a lot about heaven. If Jesus wants us to think about heaven, you know the enemy does NOT want us to think about heaven. The enemy is opposed to us living powerful lives here. He wants you to just think about yourself and your comfort here and now.

What Does The Bible Say About Heaven?

In order to distract us from the truth, the enemy has planted into our world some myths and stories about what heaven might be like. Most of the myths have to do with big locked gates, clouds, hearts, and angels that look like babies with wings. These images and ideas distract us from thinking about the reality of heaven. They make it harder for us to obey the Bible and set our eyes on the things of heaven. Thankfully, God put a ton of information in the Bible about heaven. The Bible is our standard of truth. God put everything we need to know in the Bible.

My goal is to give you just a little bit of an idea of what heaven is like. I want to tell you what the Bible says about where heaven is (both now, and after Jesus finishes his plan for getting rid of evil), who is in heaven right now, and what our bodies will be like in heaven. If I can start you out on the right track with these basic truths, you will be able to start developing a "holy imagination" about heaven and your life beyond what you can see. This is so important! We need to get in the habit of asking the Holy Spirit to reveal to us ideas about our lives in heaven. We want our dreams to extend beyond this age. You need your imagination for this! God designed us with an imagination. He wants us to begin setting our eyes on the things above. The only way to do that is fueling our imagination by the truth of His word.

Where Heaven Is

First, let's start with where heaven is right now. This is actually pretty easy to answer. Check out what the Bible says in Acts:

> *(Act 1:9-11) After saying this, he was taken up to heaven as they watched him, and a cloud hid him from their sight. They still had their eyes fixed on the sky as he went away, when two men dressed in white suddenly stood beside them and said, "Galileans, why are you standing there looking up at the sky? This*

Jesus, who was taken from you into heaven, will come back in the same way that you saw him go to heaven."

Right now heaven is "up." It is outside of our atmosphere, and maybe outside of our universe. Every time we read in the Bible about someone, a person or an angel, going to heaven, they go "up." Every time we read about a person or angel coming from heaven to earth, they go "down." An even better answer to this question is that heaven is where God is. Right now, God the Father and Jesus are "up" in heaven. The spirits of people that have died, and trusted that Jesus paid the price for their sins when He died on the cross, are with God right now. Paul told the Church in Corinth this truth:

(2 Corinthians 5:8) Yes, we are fully confident, and we would rather be away from these earthly bodies, for then we will be at home with the Lord.

Who Is There?

Your spirit is everything that makes you who you are. Your memory, your thoughts, your opinions, your likes, and dislikes, your love, your passion...these belong to you forever. They may change over time, but they are yours. When someone on earth dies, their body may decay in the ground, but their spirit continues on. If you have a saving knowledge of Jesus, when you die, your spirit goes to be with God in heaven. This is a glorious truth! Look at what Jesus told the repentant thief on the cross next to Him:

(Luke 23:42-43)   Then he said, "Jesus, remember me when You come into Your Kingdom." And Jesus replied, "I assure you, today you will be with Me in paradise."

Heaven, or paradise, is a real location. God has His throne there right now. Redeemed humans live there right now. Revelation Chapter 4 describes in great detail God's throne, who is there, what it looks like, and where it is. It is important that you know all of these details. You should read Revelation Chapter 4 often. It helps us to focus on the reality of God's location and His intentions for people and angels. When you read Revelation 4, you quickly realize God loves to be in the presence of His creation. He has surrounded His throne with angels and people. There is a great crystal sea in front of His throne. This sea is made for His people to stand on in His presence (Revelation 7:9).   You can access this throne even now, before you die. When Jesus paid the price on the cross for us, He made a way for our spirits to go before God's throne. Look at what Hebrews 4:16 says:

(Hebrews 4:16) So let us come boldly to the throne of our gracious God. There we will receive His mercy, and we will find grace to help us when we need it most.

When we pray, our spirit, everything that makes us who we are, goes before God's actual throne. Our bodies stay right here on earth, but our spirit appears before Him in heaven. This is an amazing truth.   The same thing happens when we worship with songs.   In those moments when you can really focus on God during worship, your spirit is actually standing before God's throne. This has huge implications for how we think about God, and heaven, and those who have gone before us to be with God. The sea of glass is where we all go to worship God. Is someone you love in heaven right now? You can stand with them in your spirit and worship God together.

We really want to focus on God during worship. You can ask the Holy Spirit to help you focus on God during worship. Just singing songs is different than allowing our spirit to travel and stand before God. We are easily distracted by what is happening around us on earth, but if we resist distraction and focus on God, everything changes. It is so important to start picturing heaven and God's throne. This is why He described where He is and what He looks like in such great detail. He wants us to start imagining Him, picturing Him, and placing our spirits before Him!

Heaven on Earth

Right now heaven is "up," but soon, heaven itself will come to earth. This is the amazing reality Jesus revealed to John in the Book of Revelation. The prophets of old understood this truth, as well. While the modern Church usually thinks of heaven being in the supernatural spirit realm, Israel has always thought of the Messiah as a man who would reign as a human king on a renewed earth. This is part of the reason they didn't recognize Jesus when He appeared on earth. The Jewish idea of the Messiah was of an earthly king that God's people would rule the earth with. The truth about heaven, and Jesus' plans for people, is a combination of both of these ideas (Ephesians 1:10; Revelation 21:2).

When Jesus comes at the last trumpet, He will defeat the antichrist, He will lock up satan for 1,000 years, and He will begin renewing the earth. This is called **the Millennium**. We will get to work with Him as He accomplishes His plan to make all things new. Jesus created the heavens and the earth in Genesis 1. Look at what God said about what He had created:

(Genesis 1:31) Then God looked over all He had made, and He saw that it was very good! And evening passed and morning came, marking the sixth day.

God's original intentions for us were "very good," and they have not changed. Once satan is locked up, those who belong to the Lord experience the "first resurrection." This sets the stage for Jesus to start renewing everything on earth. The Bible promises we are blessed if we take part in this first resurrection. Death is no longer a possibility for us, and we will be representatives (kings and priests) of God on earth with Jesus. Look at what it says in Revelation 20:

(Revelation 20:3-6) The angel threw him into the bottomless pit, which he then shut and locked so Satan could not deceive the nations anymore until the thousand years were finished. Afterward he must be released for a little while. Then I saw thrones, and the people sitting on them had been given the authority to judge. And I saw the souls of those who had been beheaded for their testimony about Jesus and for proclaiming the word of God. They had not worshiped the beast or his statue, nor accepted his mark on their forehead or their hands. They all came to life again, and they reigned with Christ for a thousand years. This is the first resurrection. (The rest of the dead did not come back to life until the thousand years had ended.) Blessed and holy are those who share in the first resurrection. For them the second death holds no

power, but they will be priests of God and of Christ and will reign with him a thousand years.

After reading that, you might be tempted to think only those who were beheaded for Jesus are raised first, but that is not exactly what the passage says. When you combine this passage with others, including what Paul told the Church in Corinth, you get a fuller picture of who reins with Jesus during the 1,000 year Millennium:

> *(1 Corinthians 15:23)   But there is an order to this resurrection: Christ was raised as the first of the harvest; then all who belong to Christ will be raised when He comes back.*

As followers of Jesus, we have an amazing privilege: we will help Jesus renew the earth for 1,000 years! What an awesome job! Can you imagine 1,000 years where there is no satan or his demons to cause trouble? Can you imagine 1,000 years where the atmosphere of the earth is actually changed back to what it was in the Garden of Eden (Revelation 21:1)? Can you imagine working with Jesus to rebuild all that was damaged in the wars and Tribulation described in the Book of Revelation? Look at what the prophet Isaiah said about the renewal of the earth:

> *(Isaiah 35:1-10) Even the wilderness and desert will be glad in those days. The wasteland will rejoice and blossom with spring crocuses.   Yes, there will be an abundance of flowers and singing and joy! The deserts will become as green as the mountains of Lebanon, as lovely as Mount Carmel or the plain of Sharon. There*

the LORD will display His glory, the splendor of our God. With this news, strengthen those who have tired hands, and encourage those who have weak knees. Say to those with fearful hearts, "Be strong, and do not fear, for your God is coming to destroy your enemies. He is coming to save you."

And when He comes, He will open the eyes of the blind and unplug the ears of the deaf. The lame will leap like a deer, and those who cannot speak will sing for joy! Springs will gush forth in the wilderness, and streams will water the wasteland. The parched ground will become a pool, and springs of water will satisfy the thirsty land. Marsh grass and reeds and rushes will flourish where desert jackals once lived. And a great road will go through that once deserted land. It will be named the Highway of Holiness. Evil-minded people will never travel on it. It will be only for those who walk in God's ways; fools will never walk there. Lions will not lurk along its course, nor any other ferocious beasts. There will be no other dangers. Only the redeemed will walk on it. Those who have been ransomed by the LORD will return. They will enter Jerusalem singing, crowned with everlasting joy. Sorrow and mourning will disappear, and they will be filled with joy and gladness.

Reading about the earth after Jesus returns can get confusing. Did you notice the sentence about the "Highway of Holiness"? It says evil-minded people will never travel it. This confused me before I really studied what the Bible says about heaven. I had always thought that there would be no evil-minded people after Jesus came and defeated the enemy! When I began studying the full description of earth after Jesus' return, I started to get a fuller picture of what the earth looks like during the Millennium.

The passage from Isaiah 35 is describing the 1,000-year renewing of the earth by Jesus. There are 3 types of people on earth when Jesus appears in the sky at the Second Coming. The *redeemed* are those who have trusted in Jesus for salvation. The redeemed are "raptured" when Jesus returns and are given their new bodies right away. There are also people who decide to worship the antichrist and take the mark of the Beast. These people, we will call them the *reprobate*, are judged along with the antichrist and are thrown into the lake of fire. Then there is a third group of people who we are usually less clear about. They are the unsaved survivors of the Tribulation who refused to worship the Antichrist. They have not trusted Jesus for salvation, but they also resisted the antichrist's domination. We will call them *resistors*. Resistors will have the opportunity to experience salvation after Jesus returns. They will populate the millennial earth. There are a ton of verses that describe the resistors. A few of them are: Isaiah 4:3, 10:20, 11:10, 65:8, and 66:19; Ezekiel 36:36; Joel 2:32; and Zechariah 14:16-21.

At the time that Jesus begins renewing the earth, there will be a renewing of Jerusalem, we'll call it the "Millennial Jerusalem." This can be confusing when you read about heaven in the Book of Revelation. You have to know there is a difference between the "New Jerusalem" and the "Millennial Jerusalem." The New Jerusalem descends out of heaven to the renewed earth at the end of the Millennium, after satan and death, and all those who rebel against Jesus are thrown into the lake of fire. Before the renewing of the earth, the

New Jerusalem descends part of the way to earth. Revelation 21:2 and Revelation 21:10 describe how the New Jerusalem descends two times. The New Jerusalem is the city where God will place His throne on earth!

The Bible does not use the term "Millennial Jerusalem," but there are at least four reasons that we can know New Jerusalem is different from the Millennial Jerusalem. First, the kings of the earth come into a glorified (Millennial) Jerusalem during the Millennium to bring their glory, honor, and wealth (Rev. 21:24). Second, the leaves of the trees along the River of Life in the Millennial Jerusalem are "for the healing of the nations" (Rev. 22:2). Healing won't be necessary in the time that God's throne is on earth and all people have resurrected bodies that don't get sick. Third, the angels guard sinners from entry (Rev. 21:12, 22:14-15) to the Millennial Jerusalem. There won't be any sinners left on earth when God's throne is in the New Jerusalem. Fourth, the Millennial Jerusalem lights up the saved nations on the millennial earth (not unsaved ones) (Rev. 21:24; 20:7-9).

We will be Jesus' partners in restoring the earth to the conditions of the Garden of Eden. We will live in the heavenly city and go out to work in the earth (Revelation 21:27). Jesus' plan is to make the earth a place for us to live everyday with God the Father, as He originally intended it to be. The Bible says this will take 1,000-years to accomplish. At the end of the 1,000 years, Jesus lets satan loose for a little while. Satan deceives and rallies the unsaved people with natural bodies on earth at that time, and they rebel against Jesus. Look at how the Bible describes the last rebellion:

(Revelation 20:7-10) When the thousand years come to an end, Satan will be let out of his prison. He will go

out to deceive the nations—called Gog and Magog—in every corner of the earth. He will gather them together for battle—a mighty army, as numberless as sand along the seashore.   And I saw them as they went up on the broad plain of the earth and surrounded God's people and the beloved city. But fire from heaven came down on the attacking armies and consumed them. Then the devil, who had deceived them, was thrown into the fiery lake of burning sulfur, joining the beast and the false prophet. There they will be tormented day and night forever and ever.

At this time, satan, death, the grave, and all those whose names are not written in the Book of Life will be thrown into the lake of fire.   The earth is purged of sin and death, and has been made ready for God the Father's throne to be moved to earth.   Check out what the Bible says:

(Revelation 21:1-5)   Then I saw a new heaven and a new earth, for the old heaven and the old earth had disappeared. And the sea was also gone.   And I saw the holy city, the new Jerusalem, coming down from God out of heaven like a bride beautifully dressed for her husband. I heard a loud shout from the throne, saying, "Look, God's home is now among His people! He will live with them, and they will be His people. God Himself will be with them.   He will wipe every tear from their eyes, and there will be no more death or sorrow or crying or pain. All these things are gone forever."   And the One sitting on the throne said, "Look, I am making everything new!" And then He said to me, "Write this down, for what I tell you is trustworthy and true."

Our Heavenly Bodies

In the Garden of Eden, God spent time with Adam and Eve face to face (Genesis 3:8). God's intention for people has always been that we would be His family. He has always wanted us to be able to spend time with Him and enjoy His presence. God wants all of the amazing wonder of the supernatural spiritual realm to be joined with all the amazing wonder of the natural realm. Human life on earth, our work, our physical gatherings, our natural senses like taste, touch, and smell...God called these "very good." We were originally created and designed to live in a physical world that God called "very good!" Right now, our loved ones in heaven have a spiritual body, because they don't need a physical body to relate the environment in heaven, but when Jesus returns at the last trumpet, and He raptures us into His presence in the sky, He will give us new resurrected bodies, just like His. Look at what the Bible says:

> *(Romans 8:23)   And we believers also groan, even though we have the Holy Spirit within us as a foretaste of future glory, for we long for our bodies to be released from sin and suffering. We, too, wait with eager hope for the day when God will give us our full rights as His adopted children, including the new bodies He has promised us.*

The apostle Paul said that new bodies are the right of everyone who is saved by Jesus. That is what it means to be adopted as God's children, to tell God that we trust that Jesus paid for our sins when He died on the cross. Just like us, people in Paul's time wanted to know what their bodies might be like. Check out what Paul said:

> *(1 Corinthians 15:42-49) It is the same way with the resurrection of the dead. Our earthly bodies are planted in the ground when we die, but they will be raised to live forever. Our bodies are buried in brokenness, but they will be raised in glory. They are buried in weakness, but they will be raised in strength. They are buried as natural human bodies, but they will be raised as spiritual bodies. For just as there are natural bodies, there are also spiritual bodies. The Scriptures tell us, "The first man, Adam, became a living person." But the last Adam—that is, Christ—is a life-giving Spirit. What comes first is the natural body, then the spiritual body comes later. Adam, the first man, was made from the dust of the earth, while Christ, the second Man, came from heaven. Earthly people are like the earthly man, and heavenly people are like the heavenly Man. Just as we are now like the earthly man, we will someday be like the heavenly Man.*

So Paul said we are not only getting a new body, but a new kind of body, a heavenly one. It will be stronger than our body now. It will have spiritual, or supernatural, capabilities that we don't have now. Remember how the Bible said that God is going to bring heaven and earth together? Heaven requires a spiritual body, and earth requires a physical "flesh and bone" body. Heaven-on-earth will require a different kind of body! You might be wondering: what will my new body be like? Paul said our new body will be like Jesus' new body. The

Bible talks about Jesus appearing to His disciples in His new body. Check it out:

> *(Luke 24:36-43) And just as they were telling about it, Jesus Himself was suddenly standing there among them. "Peace be with you," He said. But the whole group was startled and frightened, thinking they were seeing a ghost! "Why are you frightened?" He asked. "Why are your hearts filled with doubt? Look at My hands. Look at My feet. You can see that it's really Me. Touch Me and make sure that I am not a ghost, because ghosts don't have bodies, as you see that I do." As He spoke, He showed them His hands and His feet. Still they stood there in disbelief, filled with joy and wonder. Then He asked them, "Do you have anything here to eat?" They gave Him a piece of broiled fish, and He ate it as they watched.*

Jesus' new body sounds pretty different from the one He had before He was raised from the dead, but also kind of the same! Let's think about what we can learn from this part of the book of Luke.

- Jesus "appeared" suddenly. He didn't need to go through doors. He could just be somewhere!
- The disciples recognized Him, but He also looked different. The disciples thought He might be a ghost. The Bible says elsewhere that our bodies are going to be glorified. We get to share in some measure of Jesus' glory, and we might be "brighter."

- The disciples could touch Jesus. In the Bible, it says Jesus' body was flesh and bone, just like we have flesh and bones now, except, Jesus' flesh and bones are not like the old flesh that could die and get sick. Jesus' new flesh and bones were perfect, the way God intended when He called creation "very good."
- Jesus ate. In our new bodies, we will still enjoy the awesome parts about earth like smells, and colors, and tastes!

Right now Jesus is the only person in heaven with a resurrected body, but soon, all of His brothers and sisters will receive their new bodies, when heaven comes to earth with Jesus. We will need these new bodies to relate to the new environment that Jesus brings to earth, the supernatural spirit realm joined to a Garden of Eden-like earth.

Holy Imagination

It is so important that we spend time thinking about and imagining what life will be like during the Millennium and in the New Jerusalem. Heaven will not be a boring endless float on a cloud with a harp. It won't be a bunch of people wandering from sanctuary to sanctuary in white robes singing hymns all day. Can you imagine exploring the world in your new body? Can you imagine spending time in a perfect paradise, eating and laughing with your friends? How about building and creating things with a renewed body in a renewed earth?

We want to start having a conversation with God about life in heaven. We can ask the Holy Spirit to begin giving us ideas about what heaven will be like for us! Ask God to give you ideas about where you will live, who you will see, and what you will do. Imagine where you will spend your time. God loves to reveal these things to our hearts. He loves for us to be excited about our future with Him. He is excited about it too!

The life God has planned for us is so amazing and perfectly fulfilling. If we spend time focusing on life with Jesus, we will naturally start living with real expectation of our time with Him, and our choices on this dying earth will reflect that! Jesus is coming soon. I don't want to meet Him with regret that I didn't give Him more when I could have! Getting ready to meet Jesus soon, and imagining living with Him forever, will actually strengthen us. Obeying the Bible and "setting our hearts on the things above" will help us get the whole world ready to live through Jesus' plan to get rid of evil on the planet!

Authority: Resist and Enemy Will Flee! - 6

Darkness is increasing all around us, but the Bible promises light will also increase. This explains why the prophet Joel called Jesus' return the "Great and Terrible Day of the Lord." As satan furiously tries to prevent the world from inviting Jesus to come, God is preparing us to be Jesus' pure and spotless bride. It is tempting for us to think that this war is fought and won in the spiritual realm, and we are some sort of earth-bound cheerleaders. This could not be further from the truth!

In the Bible, Paul described us as "more than conquerors." He was telling the Church that, because of what Jesus had done for us on the cross, and God's love for us, we would overcome anything that opposed us in our relationship with God. Check out what Paul said in Romans:

(Romans 8:29-31)   For God knew His people in advance, and He chose them to become like His Son, so that His Son would be the firstborn among many brothers and sisters.   And having chosen them, He called them to come to Him. And having called them, He gave them right standing with Himself. And having given them right standing, He gave them His glory. What shall we say about such wonderful things as these? If God is for us, who can ever be against us?

Paul was revealing a deep truth: we are in a position of great authority in the world. He was explaining to the Church that because of our standing, or our family position in God's kingdom, we were equipped to stand against the enemy. As the birth pangs Jesus described at the end of the age become more intense, standing against darkness is going to become more and more important in our lives. The great news is we don't have to wait for darkness to increase any more before we start increasing the light! In fact, there is a great opportunity before us right now to take back territory from the enemy and establish "lighthouses" all around our cities. The power to overcome is in the name of Jesus! This requires some explaining, but you must be confident about how and why uttering Jesus' amazing name changes things in heaven and on earth. Before we go any further, take a minute and ask the Holy Spirit to guide you into this truth, in Jesus' name!

What most people don't realize is that Jesus did a lot more than buy you and me a ticket to heaven when He died on the cross and rose again. Don't get me wrong, the fact that He DID buy us a ticket to heaven is awesome, but the truth is He did much more than that. He redeemed us, and all of creation. This is a big statement. For you to start to understand how big it is, you really have to know what the word redeem means. Redeem simply means to "buy back." Think soda cans for a second. When you buy a soda at the store, if you live where I live, you pay 10 cents for the can in addition to whatever the soda costs. When you are done with the can, you bring it back to the store, and they redeem the can. The store buys the can back for 10 cents. Jesus redeemed, or "bought back," all of creation.

The Law of Redemption

When Jesus lived a perfect and sinless life, and then was crucified on a cross, He redeemed all of creation (Romans 8:21) from sin and satan. It was a legal transaction. Heaven is governed by laws, and God likes order. He made things to work a certain way. All things seen and unseen, like gravity and chemistry, have to obey God's order. When things get out of order it causes chaos, and there are consequences. The Bible says that even human authorities, like policemen who maintain order in the natural realm, are established by God. Check out what the apostle Paul wrote to the Church in Rome:

> *(Romans 13:1-2) Everyone must submit to governing authorities. For all authority comes from God, and those in positions of authority have been placed there by God. So anyone who rebels against authority is rebelling against what God has instituted, and they will be punished.*

God is serious about order.   When Adam and Eve rebelled against God by believing satan instead of God, God's order for all of creation was violated.   There were big consequences. The biggest was a separation of people from God. God created us to be His eternal companion, but our rebellion got in the way. Don't worry, there is good news! God loves us so much that He had written into the laws of creation a way to redeem people! We'll call it the "Law of Redemption."

In the Old Testament God gave the Israelites laws to live by. Do you remember the story of God giving Moses the 10 Commandments (you can find these in Exodus 20)? Moses carried these basic laws for God's people down the mountain after receiving them directly from God. Along with the 10 Commandments, God gave Moses several other laws, one of which was the Law of Redemption. You can read the Law of

Redemption in Leviticus 25. I have paraphrased it below to make it a little easier to follow:

> *(Leviticus 25:47-50 paraphrased) Suppose one of you owes some money and is forced to sell themselves as a slave, they still can be bought back, even after they have become a slave. They may be bought back by a brother, an uncle, or a cousin. In fact, anyone from their family may buy them back. They may also redeem themselves if they can afford it. They will negotiate the price of their freedom with the person who bought them. The price will be based on whatever it would cost to hire a worker for as long as they are to be a slave.*

Now, from what you just read, answer these two questions:

1. Who has the right to buy back the person who is a slave? (answer: Someone who is their family)
2. What is the price to be paid to buy someone back out of slavery? (answer: Whatever their lives are worth for the time they had left to be a slave)

When Adam and Eve believed satan, and trusted what he said over what God said, they sold themselves as slaves to sin for the rest of their lives. Ultimately this slavery was a death sentence ending in eternal separation from God. What's more, Adam and Eve's kids were born as the children of two slaves, and were slaves themselves! Since all of mankind is related to Adam and Eve, this went on and on, and on, and on.

The only right of redemption for people was found in the Law of Redemption written into creation by God himself. According to the law, for us to be free of slavery, we would need a relative born outside of our sin-enslaved condition who could pay the price for the remainder of our lives in slavery. Are you wondering what the price for sin is? Check out what it says in Romans 6:23:

> *(Romans 6:23) For the wages of sin is death, but the free gift of God is eternal life through Christ Jesus our Lord.*

The Price Paid for Sin

Money can't buy our way out of sin, even being good can't make up for our sin, the Bible says only death can pay the price for sin. For a long time after Adam and Eve sold themselves into slavery, people, starting with Adam's son Able (Genesis 4:4), offered animal sacrifices to try to pay for their sins. The death of animals was used to pay for the sins of people. This was only a temporary way pointing to the perfect way God had to put things back into order. Do you think animals are worth the same amount as a person? What about all the animals in the world, are their lives worth one person? Not according to the Bible. Check out what God says in Hebrews 10:4?

> *(Hebrews 10:4) For it is not possible for the blood of bulls and goats to take away sins.*

But God had a plan. He knew we needed a perfect human, someone who wasn't born as a slave to sin, and who could live a perfect and sinless life, to pay the wages of sin with His own death. An innocent man willing to give up His life could fulfill the Law of Redemption, and bring people back into the order God intended for us. God also knew that no son or daughter of Adam and Eve could be born free of sin's grip. He knew only a perfect human, His own Son, could pay the price for us. God revealed to many of the prophets bits and pieces of His amazing plan to send Jesus to redeem us, but one of the most amazing prophecies was one He gave to the prophet Daniel. You have to see what it says:

> *(Daniel 7:13-14) As my vision continued that night, I saw someone like a son of man coming with the clouds of heaven. He approached the Ancient One and was led into His presence. He was given authority, honor, and sovereignty over all the nations of the world, so that people of every race and nation and language would obey Him. His rule is eternal—it will never end. His kingdom will never be destroyed.*

The Son of Man

"Son of Man" is a very important phrase in Daniel 7:13. In fact, this is the name Jesus used most to refer to Himself throughout the Gospels. If you have spent much time reading the Gospels, you have certainly seen this title for Jesus numerous times. It is a weird title, but it is extremely important. By using this reference to Daniel's vision, Jesus communicated to the religious leaders exactly who He was and why He had come. In fact, I want you to lock this name for Jesus in your mind.

Let me explain. The next verse in this passage, Daniel 7:15, says that Daniel was disturbed by the vision he had seen. The vision was regarding the end of the age, and there was a lot of disturbing imagery associated with it, but I think Daniel was disturbed by more than what was going to happen in the future. Since Adam and Eve rebelled against God, no human eyes had ever looked at God again. In fact, Daniel would have known about this conversation that God had with Moses in Exodus 33 18:20:

> *(Exodus 33:18-20) Moses responded, "Then show me Your glorious presence." The LORD replied, "I will make all My goodness pass before you, and I will call out My name, Yahweh, before you. For I will show mercy to anyone I choose, and I will show compassion to anyone I choose. But you may not look directly at My face, for no one may see Me and live."*

Moses had a relationship with God like no one else. God said He spoke to Moses "face to face" (Exodus 33:11), but even Moses could not see God and live. This is because God's holiness makes him so bright that it would kill you to see Him in your current human body (this was a consequence of sin brought on by Adam and Eve's rebellion). Check out what it says in 1 Timothy 6:16:

> *(1 Timothy 6:16) He alone can never die, and he lives in light so brilliant that no human can approach him. No human eye has ever seen him, nor ever will. All honor and power to him forever! Amen.*

Can you imagine a light so bright you couldn't come near it? Have you ever tried looking right at the sun on a sunny day? You shouldn't do it! It will hurt your eyes. God created the sun and it is nothing compared to HIS brightness. Have you ever wondered why God is invisible to us? Have you ever thought "God, if you are real, why don't you just let us see you?" I have thought that before. Daniel, like all of us, certainly considered this as well. Daniel knew the scriptures (Daniel 9:2) and would have known man could not see God and live. Now, all of the sudden, Daniel was seeing a vision of a man...a human being...in a human body, standing before God the Father (the Ancient One).   This was certainly disturbing and perplexing to Daniel.

Jesus was the man Daniel was seeing in the vision. For Daniel, it was a vision of the future.   For us, it was an historic event. It was a picture of Jesus receiving His inheritance after His resurrection. He was completing the transaction of his redeeming payment. You see, Jesus is the perfect and sinless man that we needed to redeem us. I can't explain this any better than the author of Hebrews did, check it out:

> *(Hebrews 2:14-17) Because God's children are human beings—made of flesh and blood—the Son also became flesh and blood. For only as a human being could He die, and only by dying could He break the power of the devil, who had the power of death. Only in this way could He set free all who have lived their lives as slaves to the fear of dying. We also know that the Son did not come to help angels; He came to help the descendants of Abraham.   Therefore, it was necessary for Him to be made in every respect like us, His brothers and sisters, so that He could be our*

merciful and faithful High Priest before God. Then He could offer a sacrifice that would take away the sins of the people.

Jesus, who was God and was with God (John 1:1) at the time of creation, watched Adam and Eve rebel against God. God the Father revealed His plan to redeem us, and Jesus agreed to do the Father's will. Jesus agreed to become a man!... Forever! (this should wreck your brain for at least a few minutes).   That is how much He loves us. He remained fully God but became FULLY man. He is the person of God who chose to put on flesh and live within the limitations of being a man. Daniel was seeing this man, the firstborn of many (Romans 8:29), in a resurrected body capable of being before the Father. It is astonishing that Jesus would humble Himself for us in this way, but this is how passionate God is about being with you. Someday, all who have put their trust in Jesus as Savior will receive a resurrected body capable of being in front of the Father, just like Jesus. This is what Jesus being the "firstborn of many" means. Jesus restored what had always been God's intention for you. He has always wanted you to be with Him. Look at Jesus' passion to be with you in John 17, just before He paid the price for your sin on the cross:

(John 17:19) And I give Myself as a holy sacrifice for them so they can be made holy by Your truth.

(John 17:24)   Father, I want these whom You have given Me to be with Me where I am. Then they can see all the glory You gave Me because You loved Me even before the world began!

All Authority Belongs To Jesus, The King

In doing all this, Jesus did pay our way back to heaven, but remember I said there was more! When Jesus stood before God and received His inheritance, He didn't just get His people back. Daniel witnessed Jesus receiving much more! Daniel said he watched the Son of Man receive authority, honor, and sovereignty over all the nations of the world. This leaves us with a question: if Jesus received all this authority and power at the time of His resurrection, who had it before Him? In order to answer that question, we have to follow the "chain of ownership" for the earth. When God made the earth, He created Adam and Eve as the first people. Listen to what God said when He made people in Genesis 1:27-28 (this is the King James Version):

> (Genesis 1:27-28) (KJV) So God created man in his own image, in the image of God created he him; male and female created he them. And God blessed them, and God said unto them, Be fruitful, and multiply, and replenish the earth, and subdue it: and have dominion over the fish of the sea, and over the fowl of the air, and over every living thing that moves upon the earth.

Did you hear what God said? He said He made people to fill the earth and subdue it, that means take it over and control it. Then, God said people would have dominion over the earth. That really just means that He gave control of the earth to humans. When God made us, He gave us the earth so that we could rule over it in partnership with Him. This was the privilege of Adam and Eve until they rebelled against God's leadership. Their rebellious act was doing the one thing they were not supposed to do: they ate the fruit they weren't supposed to eat.   When they ate the fruit, they actually rebelled against God's leadership and trusted satan's leadership instead.   When Adam and Eve rebelled against God's leadership and aligned with satan, they handed over their ownership of the earth to the devil! Satan himself stated this to Jesus. Look at Luke 4:5-7:

> *(Luke 4:5-7) Then the devil took Him up and revealed to Him all the kingdoms of the world in a moment of time.   "I will give You the glory of these kingdoms and authority over them," the devil said, "because they are mine to give to anyone I please.   I will give it all to You if You will worship me."*

Satan was given control of the earth by Adam and Eve when they rebelled against God. They became slaves of sin, and the devil took what God had given Adam and Eve. However, when God gave humans the earth, He **really** meant it! He had a plan to restore the ownership of the earth to humans. The plan was for His very own Son, Jesus, who was God, and was with the Father, to become a human, and live a perfect life as a man. He did this so He could qualify to redeem humans from sin and death. Jesus lived His earthly life as a human perfectly aligned with the Father's leadership. Because of Jesus' perfect obedience and unjust death, He not only paid the price for our sins, He actually won back control of the earth as a man! Jesus receiving His inheritance was what Daniel saw in his vision. Now, through the man Jesus, the earth is back in control of humans. Look at what Jesus said in Matthew 28:18-20 when He spoke to His disciples after His resurrection from death:

(Matthew 28:18-20) "Jesus came and told His disciples, "I have been given all authority in heaven and on earth. Therefore, go and make disciples of all the nations, baptizing them in the name of the Father and the Son and the Holy Spirit. Teach these new disciples to obey all the commands I have given you. And be sure of this: I am with you always, even to the end of the age."

Jesus knew he was winning back the world for humans before He paid the price for us on the cross. The earth is His and someday He is coming back to drive evil off of His planet. Until then, He has left us in charge of enforcing His victory in His name. You see, Jesus said that the devil was a thief, and until He is locked up, satan and his demons continue to try to steal authority from Jesus' kingdom. That is why Jesus taught the apostles to resist the devil and the demons. Look at what the apostle James said:

(James 4:7) So then, submit yourselves to God. Resist the Devil, and he will run away from you.

The Authority of Jesus' Body

Now get this: the devil knows Jesus beat him at the cross, but He is counting on the fact that you don't know that! The Bible says when Jesus rose from the dead, He made a spectacle of the devil and the demons. Check out what Paul said in Colossians:

(Colossians 2:14-15) He canceled the record of the charges against us and took it away by nailing it to the cross. In this way, He disarmed the spiritual rulers and

authorities. He shamed them publicly by His victory over them on the cross.

Paul was saying Jesus shamed them publicly in the spiritual realm. Here in the natural realm, most people had no idea what had happened. Jesus is in control of everything. Listen to what Paul said about Jesus:

(Ephesians 1:21-23)   Christ rules there above all heavenly rulers, authorities, powers, and lords; he has a title superior to all titles of authority in this world and in the next.   God put all things under Christ's feet and gave him to the Church as supreme Lord over all things. The Church is Christ's body, the completion of him who himself completes all things everywhere.

Did you hear that!   Jesus rules over everything! Including the devil, demons, angels, world leaders, all the stars and   planets...everything!   However,   although   Jesus "disarmed" His enemies and has authority over everything, His enemies haven't been locked up yet.   This is the key to understanding the trouble we face.

Although the devil and his demons still attempt to steal Jesus' kingdom authority, for people who belong to Jesus, the enemies are like toothless lions.   Satan may make a lot of noise, but for those of us that belong to the Kingdom, he has no teeth.   When we resist the enemy, like the Bible tells us to, they must give up their stolen authority.

Paul said something we have to hear in verse 23.   He basically said "Jesus is the head and we are His body."   Now, when your head thinks of something that needs doing, like brushing your teeth, does your head pick up the toothbrush and start brushing? No, you need your hand for that. The body does what the head wants done. This is where we come in. This is why James said to resist the devil, and why Jesus trained His disciples to cast out demons and heal people (Luke 10). Our job is to resist the enemy, because Jesus wants us to. When we resist the enemy, we are promised the enemy must flee! Jesus has given us authority to use the power that belongs to Him. It requires the use of His name, which invokes the power of His kingdom.

To grasp this, we have to think for a minute about the difference between authority and power. Think of it like this: when a policeman stops a car, does he use power or authority? He sticks his hand up and maybe blows his whistle, and the car stops. He is using authority. If he was using power, he would have to step out in the road and try to stop the car with his body! That wouldn't go very well for the policeman! You see, a policeman has a lot of authority, even if he doesn't have a lot of power. The policeman has the authority to represent the power of the government, which ultimately relies on the strength of its military. We have the authority to represent the power of God's kingdom. This is the most powerful government in existence. The power of God that created the universe in six days and raised Jesus from the dead is the same power behind the authority of our words when we assert them in the name of Jesus, the King and Owner of all creation.

This is the part where we often get mixed up. We often ask God to resist the devil for us, but the Bible tells us it is our job to resist the devil. We might pray "God please stop the devil from doing "x" to me, in Jesus' name." Praying is always better than not praying, and I bet most of us have seen God answer prayers just like this one. God is merciful.

He honors all of our attempts to reach for Him, but we need to discern between what is good and what is best. I believe Jesus wants us to grow in our understanding about what He paid for and gave to us? He sent out 72 of His disciples to heal and cast out demons on His behalf to train them to do this work themselves, in His name (Luke 10:1). Even though Jesus was physically on earth, He sent them out on their own. They were amazed that the evil spirits obeyed them (Luke 10:17).

We need to do our part (be the body), but that requires us to let Jesus do do His part (be the head) (Ephesians 1:23). Apart from Jesus, we can do nothing. Period. However, when we are in constant communication with Jesus, and submitted to Him...remaining in Him (John 15:4), He promised we will do even greater things than He did (John 14:12).

We are Jesus' mouth on earth. The police officer doesn't call his captain to come pull cars over when he sees one speeding. The traffic officer does it himself. It is his responsibility. Jesus wants US to stop the devil with His name. This requires a spiritual maturing from asking God to take authority over the enemy as he interferes with us and those around us ("God, please make the enemy leave in Jesus' name"), to obeying the Bible and taking authority over the enemy ourselves, in the name of Jesus ("enemy leave in the name of Jesus"). My family and I have experienced breakthrough in the effectiveness of our prayers as we have begun to understand this principle. Anyone who is in Jesus' kingdom can do this!

The Devil Is a Thief

The devil is a liar and a thief. Until Jesus completes His plan to lock up satan and drive evil off the planet, satan will continue to pretend to be in authority and steal territory from Jesus.   As long as we don't resist him, the devil is free to interfere with our lives, and the lives of people we love. Here are just a few of the ways satan and his demons try to inflict their counterfeit authority upon our lives:

- They try to make us afraid by lying to us
- They sometimes can cause sickness (not all sickness is from him, but sometimes it is, like in the book of Job, or in the case of Paul's messenger of satan (2 Corinthians 12:7))
- They try to cause trouble in our relationships through pride, irritation, anxiety, jealousy, anger, etc... (the result is arguing and division)
- They try to bring depression and oppressive conditions into our emotions
- They try to tempt us to do things we know we shouldn't or don't want to do (like theft, addictions, lying, or lust)

This is by no means an exhaustive list of satan's attempts to usurp authority.   If there is strife, you can be pretty sure satan is in some way related to it. In James 4:7, James was basically saying that "when strife comes into your life, resist it." A lot of times we are tempted to think "if God allowed it, it must be part of His plan." This is a wrong understanding of God's intentions for you. Think about Jesus' own life on earth. Many sick and demon possessed people were all around Him. Jesus didn't say "the Father intended this to teach all of these people more about faith." He did the opposite. Everywhere He went, He resisted and cast out the enemy. This is what resulted in faith rising up in the land, and Jesus becoming famous. Seeing Jesus' power is the best builder of faith! Check out Mark 7:35-37:

> *(Mark 7:35-37) Instantly the man could hear perfectly, and his tongue was freed so he could speak plainly! Jesus told the crowd not to tell anyone, but the more He told them not to, the more they spread the news. They were completely amazed and said again and again, "Everything He does is wonderful. He even makes the deaf to hear and gives speech to those who cannot speak."*

We never want to accept the negative attacks as a test from God (James 1:13), or as a part of His will for us. That doesn't mean we have all the answers for why negative things happen. Negative and positive things happen to both good and bad people alike (Matthew 5:45). There may be times when God allows us to remain under persecution, but this is His prerogative. We may not understand everything that God is doing, but understanding is not a requirement for obedience!

We need to remember that it is God's job to lay out the plan for our life, and our job to follow His directions in the Word. Jesus wants partners in His people. He said we are actually His body on the face of the earth. God sees more than we do, and promises to work all things for the good of those who love Him and are called according to His purposes (Romans 8:28). God orders us to resist the enemy. This was God's command to us in James 4:7. We need to live by this simple principle: The more I enforce Jesus' victory, the more people will see God move. The less I enforce Jesus' victory, the less people see God move. Jesus really gave us work to do in His name!

Growing Faith Requires Risks

When we begin to use Jesus' authority, our faith may be weak. We need to stand on the truth of what the Bible says: when we resist the enemy, he must flee. The enemy may return, sometimes quickly, but if you will stick with resisting his attacks, you will quickly see the wisdom of trusting God in this. The more we take risks in our faith, the more our faith moves from believing to seeing. If we never take risks, we will never move from believing to seeing.

I have found that amazing things happen when we begin to enforce Jesus' victory on earth. Simply by resisting the spirit of depression, I have personally been freed from a lifelong struggle with depression. Whenever I am attacked with depressive thoughts, I say "spirit of depression, leave now in the name of Jesus." I may need to utter this phrase several times before I experience lasting relief, but I have been victorious every time I have resisted this spirit. Before I learned this principle, it was not uncommon for me to be depressed for weeks at a time. Now I am rarely affected by depression for more than hours, as long as I am willing to resist!

If you will ask the Holy Spirit to guide you in learning about actively resisting the enemy with your mouth, He will escort you deeper and deeper into this truth. It is God's desire that you take risks, and begin to build a history of victory against the devil and demons. Now is the time to begin building your history of faith. There are a couple of things we should clarify before we go any further:

1. Most of the strife we encounter is multi-faceted. For example, human conflict can be rooted in us giving in to our own fleshy temptations to be prideful, or jealous, etc. However, demonic attacks often heighten the intensity of the problem. If we will pray against a spirit of pride in a situation where pride is evident, the intensity of the conflict will die down. Then we can see more clearly and easily how to address the human elements.

2. Not all sickness is demon-related. Some sickness is caused by demonic attack, but sickness can also be caused by physiological conditions. Our job is to resist the sickness; God is the one who holds the power and knowledge of the source of sickness. Sometimes healing comes, and sometimes it doesn't. Our job is to resist the strife in our lives and the lives of those around us; God's job is to carry out His ultimate plans. We can trust His sovereignty, but we need to realize that He calls us into partnership with Him. Resisting negative attacks should not be optional in the life of a Christian.

How Does It Look In Real Life?

I want to give you a practical example and a testimony to help you picture how this can affect your life. Let's say for example you hear your mom and dad fighting. If you want to resist the enemy in that situation, all you have to do is say this "spirit who is causing this fighting (to help me focus my attack, I try to name the spirit. In this instance I would name it division. If I hear prideful statements, I would also resist a spirit of pride), go now in Jesus' name." Now we can just say that quietly, so only we can hear it, as long as we say it on earth, it is a rule that <u>must</u> be obeyed by the enemy. That is all there is to it. If someone is sick, we can actually say "headache, or stomach ache, or arm-ache, (you get the point) leave now in Jesus' name, and if there is an enemy causing this headache, I tell the enemy to leave now in Jesus' name, too!"

You see, it is Jesus' name that is above all other names. It doesn't matter if we yell it, or whisper it. The enemy HAS to do what Jesus says...and when we say it in Jesus' name, the enemy has to obey. The volume doesn't matter. You could yell commands all day long, and without Jesus' name, nothing would happen, but you could whisper a command in Jesus' name, and the spirits must move. It all has to do with ownership and authority. Right now, Jesus owns everything and has given us His authority. It matters when we actively enforce Jesus' authority as his body here on earth. Your mouth becomes his mouth when you agree with Him and resist the devil. Isn't that exciting?! The enemy might come back later to try to cause more trouble, but if we are faithful to resist them, satan and his helpers must leave every time. This is what Jesus said to His disciples:

(Matthew 18:18) "I tell you the truth, whatever you forbid on earth will be forbidden in heaven, and whatever you permit on earth will be permitted in heaven.

You can see from this verse, speaking a command on earth moves things in heaven. We also learn from this verse that our authority isn't limited to resisting the enemy. We can "permit" positive things into our lives and the lives of those we love. Some translations state this as the authority to "loose." This literally means we can let loose things like hope, or peace, or joy, or love, faithfulness, gentleness, kindness, self control. There is no limit to the positive parts of the Kingdom that we can literally "speak" into others lives. If we will not only forbid (resist) the enemy, but also let loose good things, like wisdom, revelation, or the fruit of the Holy Spirit, into the situations we encounter, we will see the light of Jesus' power dramatically push back the darkness the enemy is trying to increase. When this happens, Jesus name will become more famous around us!

When I first started learning about enforcing Jesus' victory, I wasn't sure if it was really true, or if it would really work. Thankfully, you don't need to be totally sure about something to try it! God loves it when we take risks in faith (Think of Peter stepping out of the boat to walk on water with Jesus). I was skeptical when I first began taking risks in this area, but as I started to try it out, some amazing things happened. God kept giving me more opportunities to resist the enemy. God used a couple of notable circumstances to build my faith:

First, we had a bunch of trouble in our neighborhood with kids arguing in an "unnatural" way. It was escalating to an intensity where violent threats were beginning to be voiced by some of the kids. Around the same time, a bike that was special to me was stolen! Now those sound like some things the enemy might be up to, don't they? Fighting and stealing, those are right up his alley! The more you learn to use the weapon of Jesus' name, the more you will find yourself looking for opportunities to enforce Jesus' victory.

When my family started to realize the enemy was causing trouble in our neighborhood, we started to take authority over the enemy causing the division in the relationships between the kids in the neighborhood. We would tell this demon to leave every time we remembered to. (A good way to build this discipline is to use the enemy's tactics against him. Usually strife is intended to create worry in our lives, and tear down faith. When you are tempted to worry go on the offensive and take authority over the enemy who is driving your worry!)

Now don't get the wrong mental picture. I didn't stand out in my front yard yelling at the devil. That might have scared all the kids away, but it probably wouldn't have been very effective at repairing relationships in our neighborhood! As strife occurred, rather than worry, or get upset about it, or complain about the person causing trouble, we would take authority over the unseen enemy stirring up the negative emotions. Division seemed to be the enemy we were most often afflicted by.

Our resisting statements and our prayers to let loose peace were verbal, but only our family knew we were using our authority. No one really needs to know but you and Jesus, and if you say it out loud, even in a whisper, it becomes an order on earth, and the enemy has to listen and obey Jesus. After a couple of days of us actively resisting the enemy, and letting loose peace, everything calmed down and all of the friends in our neighborhood started getting along again. God was giving us an awesome chance to partner with Him in bringing peace to our friends and neighbors! What looked like a really bad situation was being turned around by God for our good, and the good of our friends.

A few weeks later, one of my son's friends started causing more trouble.   During this time, this boy was intentionally trying to stir up division between the close friendships.   This friend's own struggle with jealousy was at work, but it was obvious something more intense was stirring up an unusual amount of trouble.   One day, while I was working in the yard, my oldest son came home from playing with his buddies and was visibly upset.   I stopped my son in the driveway to find out what had occurred.   He told me this friend had been unusually cruel, and called my son several hurtful names.

For a moment I was furious, but then I remembered everything God had been teaching me about my authority in Jesus' name.   I did my best to lay down my anger, and I said in just a whisper only I could hear, "enemy that is causing division in our neighborhood, leave now in the name of Jesus."   I also told God that I gave up my right to be angry at this kid and prayed peace into my own heart, in Jesus' name.   I realized my fight was with the unseen dark power at work, and not the physical mouth that spoke the mean words.

A few minutes later, the most remarkable thing happened.   The friend who had been so cruel to my son minutes earlier came walking up the driveway.   He had obviously been crying.   This boy admitted that he had been really mean and he wanted to apologize to my son.   That moment I started to realize the life changing nature of the authority Jesus had given me.   Not only did I have a tool for dealing with my own issues, I had the authority to really partner with God to positively change the lives of the people around me, and set them free from the harassment of the enemy.

Now, about this same time, my bike was stolen out of our garage one night. This bike was very special to me and was quite expensive. I worked on it a lot, and I loved to ride it. When it was stolen, I was sad and mad at the person who stole it, even though I didn't know who it was. When we called the police to report it stolen, they came to my house to investigate and take fingerprints. The police officer said I would probably not get it back, since stolen bikes are typically not recovered. God had been teaching me about the authority in Jesus' name, and I knew being mad at the thief wasn't going to accomplish anything, so I started to pray against the spirit of theft driving the person that had broken in to our garage. Every day for about three weeks I would say "enemy that made someone steal my bike, I resist you in Jesus name."

After a few weeks, I gave up praying and figured that my bike must just be gone for good (I wish I would have kept resisting!). A few more weeks passed and we went away for the weekend for a short vacation. When we were driving home from our vacation, I received a call from the police officer who had taken our theft report. He was so excited! He had found my bike, and caught the person who had it. The thief had apparently stolen numerous bikes from the neighborhood and stashed them in the woods behind his parent's house.

Most of the bikes were severely damaged from being out in the weather. However, my bike had been stored in the garage of the house. The officer said my bike was noticed by the suspect's father, who called the police when He realized his son couldn't have afforded to buy it. The police officer was amazed that I was able to get my bike back, but I wasn't. Jesus is powerful, and God was teaching me to enforce Jesus' victory on the earth! He wants you to take risks so He can build your history of victory, too!

I want to remind you of what we read in Chapter 1 about the true nature of our struggle on earth. Check out Ephesians 6:12-13:

(Ephesians 6:12-13) For we are not fighting against human beings but against the wicked spiritual forces in the heavenly world, the rulers, authorities, and cosmic powers of this dark age. So put on God's armor now! Then when the evil day comes, you will be able to resist the enemy's attacks; and after fighting to the end, you will still hold your ground.

The trouble we have with people, the trouble we have with fear, and the trouble we even have with ourselves is often caused, or made worse by, our enemy. But there is really good news: when we tell that enemy to go in Jesus' name, it must obey. Like the apostle Paul said, when we have resisted him and fought to the end, we will still hold our ground, and our enemy will have to run away! As darkness tries to increase, we can determine to what extent it will increase around us. This is part of Jesus' battle plan. As the enemy attempts to increase his resistance to Jesus' plans to return, it is going to be more and more important that we learn to operate in the way Jesus told us to. Now is the time to learn to swing this sword!

Rise of the End-Time Worship Movements - 7

Music is everywhere. At no other time in world history has music been so accessible. MP3 players, smart-phones, laptops, and other media devices have given many people access to thousands, even tens of thousands of songs, at any given time. Even live music can be watched from anywhere with a few keystrokes and the help of video-sharing websites. In the grocery store, in your car, at the mall, in the restaurant, the elevator, on hold waiting for customer service...music is literally everywhere. You could not make it through a day in most cities in America without hearing at least a portion of a song somewhere.

This is new. Because our environment changes so slowly and subtly, like a flower growing, we don't notice major cultural changes unless we really take a break and think about them. Our time in history is so unique. The rise of computer technology in the last 20 years has radically changed our access to music, video, and writing. As devices get smaller and smaller, all this information can go with us anywhere. With today's technology, an entire library's collection of music can fit on a flash memory card the size of your fingernail. At no other time in history could you watch what was happening on the other side of the world in real-time on a device as small as a smart-phone. Because of smart-phone technology, many of us carry a portal into what is currently happening everywhere in the developed world.

Is it a coincidence that technology is exploding at the same time that evil is increasing, the world economy is teetering, and the birth pangs that Jesus spoke about in

Matthew 24 are becoming more obvious? Is this all some natural occurrence that God didn't see coming? No! Look at what God revealed to the prophet Daniel in approximately 620 B.C. (that is about 2,600 years ago):

> *(Daniel 12:4) But you, Daniel, keep this prophecy a secret; seal up the book until the time of the end, when many will rush here and there, and knowledge will increase.*"

The Communication Revolution

God revealed to Daniel that at the "time of the end" knowledge would increase and many would "rush here and there." We could easily think God mentioned this to Daniel simply as a sign of the time of the end, but the "increasing of knowledge" is crucial to God's end-time plans.

The increase of knowledge we see happening all around us is related to one very specific invention: the internet.   The creation of the internet has dramatically changed everything about how people communicate.   The internet has changed how much knowledge we have access to, how quickly we can access knowledge, and how quickly we can distribute knowledge. For the first time in world history, the entire developed world can know in real-time what is happening everywhere.

A few decades ago, people received their news of what was happening in the evening the day after it happened. As cable news networks developed, the speed that news could travel to us increased, but it was still filtered by the people who delivered the news.   News networks need to sell advertising to make money, so the stories they delivered had to appeal to customers, and the companies that might want to advertise between shows. Limitations on time and resources required that news networks only produce the most appealing stories. The same was true with music on the radio, or with stories printed in books, newspapers, and magazines.

The internet has changed everything about the delivery of information. Now, anyone with a computer can deliver a story to the entire world, in minutes. Anyone with access to the internet can deliver a song to the world. Anyone with a smart-phone can film and deliver a movie to the world. The power to quickly move information to the masses has been unleashed to nearly everyone in the world for the first time in world history. This is what God revealed to Daniel would happen in the last days.

Babylon Un-paused

The internet has made possible the renewal of the "spirit of Babylon." It was this spirit that brought men together to oppose God at the Tower of Babel in Genesis 11. God wasn't worried that the Babylonians would build a really tall building! He knew that pure evil would result from a lot of people working together apart from God . In Genesis 11, God scattered the people of Babylon and confused their languages to stop this spirit. He wasn't ready to let people experience full and pure evil.

The internet has reconnected what God scattered. God knew that when left on our own, the human spirit would desire to fully rebel against God. God eventually lets people have what they want. Although in Genesis 11 He delayed man's ability to experience the fullness of rebellion from Him, the Bible says that eventually God will allow people to fully rebel against Him. The Mystery Babylon religion, which is described vividly in Revelation 17, is the result of mankind's full rebellion against God in the end.   Check out this description of this evil end-time religion:

> *(Revelation 17:1-6) One of the seven angels who had poured out the seven bowls came over and spoke to me. "Come with me," he said, "and I will show you the judgment that is going to come on the great prostitute, who rules over many waters. The kings of the world have committed adultery with her, and the people who belong to this world have been made drunk by the wine of her immorality." So the angel took me in the Spirit into the wilderness. There I saw a woman sitting on a scarlet beast that had seven heads and ten horns, and blasphemies against God were written all over it. The woman wore purple and scarlet clothing and beautiful jewelry made of gold and precious gems and pearls. In her hand she held a gold goblet full of obscenities and the impurities of her immorality. A mysterious name was written on her forehead: "Babylon the Great, Mother of All Prostitutes and Obscenities in the World." I could see that she was drunk—drunk with the blood of God's holy people who were witnesses for Jesus. I stared at her in complete amazement.*

God uses the image of a "spiritual prostitute" to convey what the Mystery Babylon is like. A prostitute sells their body for profit. Those who belong to this evil religion will do this too. They will give the sacred part of themselves, their heart, to this evil religion in order to get the great wealth, justice, and freedom it promises. People will deny the real God, and choose to serve a false idea of a god without Jesus. Many religions will join the Mystery Babylon religion, because of the unity and the good works it will be known for. Look at Revelation 17:4:

(Revelation 17:4) The woman wore purple and scarlet clothing and beautiful jewelry made of gold and precious gems and pearls. In her hand she held a gold goblet full of obscenities and the impurities of her immorality.

This one verse gives us a lot of insight into how great the Mystery Babylon will look to the world. The image of purple and scarlet clothing indicates royalty is connected to the religion. Famous people and world leaders will support and praise the Mystery Babylon religion. The beautiful jewelry that she wears indicates she will control large amounts of money. The gold cup (goblet) in her hand is a very revealing image. The gold cup indicates she will offer the world something to drink that looks very valuable: wealth, peace, and justice. But these things are not really in the cup, only fake and temporary substitutes of these things are there.

The Bible says that in her cup are "the obscenities and impurities of her immorality." This cup is filed with the fruit of a complete disconnect from God. This cup actually holds the fullness of man's rebellion: obscenity and impurity. This religion is ancient Babylon revived. God allows humans, through the technology of the internet, to press "play" on the rebellion God "paused" in Genesis 11.

The Book of Revelation reveals that the antichrist will use the Mystery Babylon religion to lead the world away from faith in the **true** Jesus. It may celebrate Jesus "the teacher" or Jesus "the prophet," but it will hate Jesus the "only savior". Under a banner of unity, this evil religion will resist people that claim Jesus is the only way to heaven. We can see the beginnings of this religion already forming. It is a humanistic social justice movement with no real connection to Jesus. It is a movement to unify all religions under a banner of political correctness, where every idea leads to heaven or enlightenment.

The Mystery Babylon is tolerant of "Christians" but hates Jesus' claim as being the only way to God. The real Jesus is offensive to this religion. There is no justice apart from Jesus. There is no peace apart from Jesus. There is no freedom apart from Jesus. But the Mystery Babylon religion promises all these things apart from Jesus. There are a couple of rallying points that the Mystery Babylon religion will center on: 1. Opposition to Israel, and 2. Opposition to Jesus as the only way of salvation (Revelation 17:6 and 17:14). The Mystery Babylon will be so intolerant of Jesus and Israel that it will eventually try to kill those who support either. What is most precious to God is most offensive to satan.

The Victorious End-Time Church

Just as the Mystery Babylon represents the total evil possible when people are united to each other without being connected to God, the Bible promises the Church will display the holiness possible when people are united to each other and connected to God's heart. The Church will experience a time of holiness and power never before seen on earth. Look at what the prophet Joel said about the end time:

> *(Joel 2:28-32)* *"Then, after doing all those things, I will pour out My Spirit upon all people. Your sons and daughters will prophesy. Your old men will dream dreams, and your young men will see visions. In those*

days I will pour out My Spirit even on servants—men and women alike.

And I will cause wonders in the heavens and on the earth—blood and fire and columns of smoke. The sun will become dark, and the moon will turn blood red before that great and terrible day of the LORD arrives. But everyone who calls on the name of the LORD will be saved, for some on Mount Zion in Jerusalem will escape, just as the LORD has said. These will be among the survivors whom the LORD has called.

Joel prophesied that even as darkness increased, God, through the pouring out of the Holy Spirit, would cause light to increase. Joel called the time when Jesus returns the "Great and Terrible Day of the Lord." That seems to be an oxymoron! Which is it: Great or Terrible?! The answer is both. This time will be great for those that know and love Jesus. It will be terrible for those that don't.

The Competing Worship Movements

The Mystery Babylon and the Victorious Church will both be fueled by powerful end-time worship movements. Worship will be offered night and day by both sides. Leaders to the end-time worship movements are rising up all over the world. People leading others in worshipping either Jesus, or social justice causes, are passionately taking their places. Large non-Jesus-based social justice protests, as well as the anthems, documentaries, and movies supporting them are popping up all over the world. So is night and day prayer and worship! Based on an internet search of the loosely affiliated Houses of Prayer (HOPs, as they are starting to be called) and "prayer furnaces", there are more than 375 HOPs, or prayer furnaces, offering some sort of night and day prayer in the United States alone!

This is just the beginning. The Bible describes the worship movements of both the Mystery Babylon, which will eventually be hijacked by the antichrist religion, and the night and day prayer and worship dedicated to Jesus. We know God wants us to worship Him, but satan feels strongly about being worshipped, as well. Check out the agreement satan tried to get Jesus to make:

> *(Matthew 4:8) Next the devil took Him to the peak of a very high mountain and showed Him all the kingdoms of the world and their glory. "I will give it all to You," he said, "if You will kneel down and worship me." "Get out of here, Satan," Jesus told him. "For the Scriptures say, 'You must worship the LORD your God and serve only Him.'"*

Many people will worship and praise satan through the Mystery Babylon religion. They will worship this religion because it will seem to offer the peace and social justice the world hungers for. This movement won't be some kind of zombie-like repeating of sentences given by the leaders; it will be passionate praise of what man can do and the "unity" of people. The music will be powerful. The worship will be from the heart, but it won't be offered to Jesus:

> *(Revelation 9:20) But the people who did not die in these plagues still refused to repent of their evil deeds and turn to God. They continued to worship demons*

*and idols made of gold, silver, bronze, stone, and
wood—idols that can neither see nor hear nor walk!*

*(Revelation 13:8) And all the people who belong to
this world worshiped the beast. They are the ones
whose names were not written in the Book of Life
before the world was made—the Book that belongs to
the Lamb who was slaughtered.*

The followers of the Mystery Babylon will at first freely
offer their worship to what seems good to them, but satan,
through the antichrist, will eventually *require* worship from
the Mystery Babylon followers. Look at what the Bible says:

*(Revelation 13:15) He was then permitted to give life
to this statue so that it could speak. Then the statue of
the beast commanded that anyone refusing to worship
it must die.*

At the same time this false worship movement is
growing, followers of Jesus will grow in wholehearted
worship, too. Worship is so important to the human spirit.
God actually wired our brains to worship, to get excited about
really good things, and think about them a lot, and spend time
daydreaming about them, singing about them, and celebrating
them. We were made to worship the really good things we
could taste, touch, see, and feel. God knew that through
worship we would get closer to what made our life really
good. When God made Adam and Eve, He was the best thing
they could see and experience on earth! This changed when
sin entered the world, and man could no longer see or
experience God face to face. Since then, man has had to fight

to keep our worship directed only towards God. In many ways, we have lost the battle.

Worship Redefined

For a lot of Christians, worship has been watered down to become "what you do to warm up the Church for the sermon." God is going to completely change our attitude about worship so we will understand worship is where we experience and release God's power. One man who really understood worship was David. David wrote a ton of worship songs and poems, called Psalms. David's Psalms are in the Bible, and we still read and sing them to this day. God proved that David knew about worship by what God said about David:

> *(Acts 13:22) But God removed Saul and replaced him with David, a man about whom God said, 'I have found David son of Jesse, a man after My own heart. He will do everything I want him to do.'*

What made David unique in his day was His strong desire to know God intimately. To know God intimately means basically to "know Him like you would know your best friend." If you get to know God intimately, you can't help but worship Him in truth! David wrote a Psalm that really says this well:

> *(Psalms 103:1-5) Let all that I am praise the LORD; with my whole heart, I will praise His holy name. Let all that I am praise the LORD; may I never forget the good things He does for me. He forgives all my sins and heals all my diseases. He redeems me from death and crowns me with love and tender mercies. He fills my*

life with good things.   My youth is renewed like the
eagle's!

David knew God was the source of every good thing in
his life, and he couldn't keep that truth inside of him. He said,
with my whole heart, I will praise God! You see, the words
that come out of our mouth tell the world what is in our heart.
Listen to what Jesus said about how our words and our heart
are connected:

> *(Mat 12:34) You brood of snakes! How could evil men*
> *like you speak what is good and right? For whatever is*
> *in your heart determines what you say.*

The Bible says what is in our heart comes out in our
words. But the Bible says the opposite is true, too. When we
worship God with our mouths, it also strengthens our heart.
Worship is crucial to Jesus' plan to get rid of evil because
worship reminds us of how amazing God is, and makes us
remember what is in His heart. Look at what Psalm 89:15-17
says:

> *(Psalm 89:15) Happy are those who hear the joyful call*
> *to worship, for they will walk in the light of Your*
> *presence, LORD.   They rejoice all day long in Your*
> *wonderful reputation. They exult in Your righteousness.*
> *You are their glorious strength. It pleases You to make*
> *us strong.*

A man named Ethan the Ezrahite wrote this Psalm.
Ethan was known as being one of the wisest men of his time
(1 Kings 4:32). He said something like this: "when I hear it is

time to worship you, God, I get really happy, because I know I am about to experience your presence. When we sing about all the good things you have done for us and how perfect you are, it makes us strong, because You make us strong."

God doesn't ask us to worship Him because He needs it. God isn't insecure about how good He is! God isn't having a bad day, or in need of us to remind Him we love Him. God knows that in worship we connect our hearts to His, and we are strengthened. When we pray with music, it opens our spirit in a unique way. Praying to music allows us to "keep our head in the game" longer and really express to God what is in our hearts. Prayer set to music, or worship, is much easier to maintain for long periods of time than just spoken prayer. This is essential as trouble increases in the world.

Biblical Descriptions of the End-Time Worship Movement

Not only will end-time worship of Jesus strengthen us to keep our gaze steady on Jesus as the world is in turmoil, it is also part of Jesus' plans to judge the antichrist empire. In partnership with us in worship, think of it as prayer set to music, Jesus will release God's judgment against the evil and oppressive antichrist world government. Many verses (i.e., Rev. 22:17; 5:8; 8:4; Lk. 18:7-8; Mt. 25:1-13; Isa. 62:6-7; 24:14-16; 5:9; 26:8-9; 27:2-5, 13; 30:18-19; 42:10-13; 43:26; 51:11; 52:8; Joel 2:12-17, 32; Jer. 31:7; Mic. 5:3-4; Zeph. 2:1-3; Ps. 102:17-20; 122:6; and Zech. 12:10) in the Bible talk about the connection between the end-time worship movement and the judgment of God being released.

This end-time Jesus worship will be the most powerful prayer and worship movement in history. Because this may be a very new concept to you, I want to highlight a few of the verses. Probably the clearest picture of the worldwide Jesus end-time worship movement can be found in the book of Isaiah. Isaiah was given a lot of insight into the end-times. Check out what he said:

> *(Isaiah 42:9-15) Everything I prophesied has come true, and now I will prophesy again. I will tell you the future before it happens."   Sing a new song to the LORD! Sing His praises from the ends of the earth! Sing, all you who sail the seas, all you who live in distant coastlands. Join in the chorus, you desert towns; let the villages of Kedar rejoice! Let the people of Sela sing for joy; shout praises from the mountaintops!*

> *Let the whole world glorify the LORD; let it sing His praise. The LORD will march forth like a mighty hero; He will come out like a warrior, full of fury. He will shout His battle cry and crush all His enemies. He will say, "I have long been silent; yes, I have restrained Myself. But now, like a woman in labor, I will cry and groan and pant. I will level the mountains and hills and blight all their greenery. I will turn the rivers into dry land and will dry up all the pools.*

This passage is describing the whole world glorifying Jesus as He marches as a mighty hero against the antichrist. It talks about singing "new songs" and Jesus' praises from the "ends of the earth." Even the far-away distant coastlands will be included. "New songs" mean prophetic, or Holy Spirit-inspired, songs will rise up across the earth. These new songs will move our hearts in powerful ways to help us walk in wholehearted obedience to Jesus and His plans. God knows that we will need spiritual strength to be steady witnesses in the face of threats from our enemies. His plan for an end-time worship movement is exactly what we will need to be the "pure and spotless bride" that the Bible describes in the end-times (Ephesians 5:27).

Another passage in Isaiah talks about music "marking the timing" of the judgments through our world-wide worship. Look at the way the Good News Translation of the Bible states it:

> (Isaiah 30:27-32) (GNT) The LORD's power and glory can be seen in the distance. Fire and smoke show his anger. He speaks, and his words burn like fire. He sends the wind in front of him like a flood that carries everything away. It sweeps nations to destruction and puts an end to their evil plans. But you, God's people, will be happy and sing as you do on the night of a sacred festival. You will be as happy as those who walk to the music of flutes on their way to the Temple of the LORD, the defender of Israel. The LORD will let everyone hear his majestic voice and feel the force of his anger. There will be flames, cloudbursts, hailstones, and torrents of rain. The Assyrians will be terrified when they hear the LORD's voice and feel the force of his punishment. As the LORD strikes them again and again, his people will keep time with the music of drums and harps. God himself will fight against the Assyrians.

Worship, or praying set to music, will be 24 hours a day, worldwide. The Church will be united in prayer and worship. Right now the internet is helping this to grow. In fact, the first modern night and day prayer started in Kansas City in 1999. Since 1999, the Kansas City International House of Prayer (IHOP-KC) has continually prayed and worshipped 24 hours a day. The internet has made it possible for others to connect with IHOP-KC from homes and smart-phones, but it has also allowed other night and day places of worship and prayer to connect prayers, music, and prophetic songs. Loosely networked Houses of Prayer are offering their own local worship and prayer, but also, when needed, drawing from others. This is just the beginning. Just as the Mystery Babylon religion will unify the streams of those opposed to Jesus, the end-time Church will be unified in praising and worshipping Jesus!

It will be the unified day and night cry to Jesus for justice that will release judgment on the antichrist and serve as a powerful witness of what God is doing. The world will see us crying out in worship and praise, and praying for the release of judgment in unity with each other worldwide. We will be organized and praying for the judgments together in the order laid out clearly in the Book of Revelation. When this happens, the world will know who is in control of the judgment, and to who they can turn for shelter. What an amazing time to be Jesus' body on earth! Look at what Jesus told His disciples about night and day worship and prayer, as He was telling them about His return:

> (Luke 18:7-8) Now, will God not judge in favor of his own people who cry to him day and night for help? Will he be slow to help them? I tell you, he will judge in their favor and do it quickly. But will the Son of Man find faith on earth when he comes?"

Our End-Time Worship Saves Our Cities

Jesus takes no pleasure in pouring out God's wrath. What He desires is this: to save the most people possible, with the least intense means possible. When other people see us as Jesus' end-time worshippers in the middle of a troubled earth, they will learn who He is, what He does, and what it all means. This is why we want to focus on building night and day worship where we live *right now*.

Earlier, we talked about Abraham's conversation with the Lord before the destruction of Sodom. The Lord told Abraham that if He could find even 10 righteous people in the city, it would be spared. How we respond to God makes a difference in our city. As evil increases, we want to be people who work for righteousness where we live. We can create a "pocket of grace" in the time of tribulation by establishing a culture of pressing into God. I want to live in a city where Jesus' people "cry out to him night and day." This is where the promise of God's favor in the end times is found.

Our efforts, as people who love Jesus and are aware of His end-time plans, should be towards establishing our city as the place where God's people cry out to Him night and day. Night and day prayer has so many benefits for a geographic area, it would be silly to try to list them all. Just consider the obvious: the unity of our local Churches, the covering of our cities in spiritual protection, the breakthrough of spiritual anointing for healing and miracles. Imagine the possibilities if your city would press into God with wholeheartedness. What kind of a witness would we be to those around us? How much more of God's power would be released in our city? As we are sheltered from judgment being released in other areas, what will people think about giving their lives to Jesus?

David knew about the power of committed worship to God for blessing a geographic area. As King of Israel, He spent an enormous amount of time and money establishing continual prayer and worship. 1 Chronicles details how David established full time worship, as directed by God. He even hired 4,000 people to serve as gatekeepers of the tabernacle, 288 professional singers, and 4,000-professional musicians to worship God. That is over 8,000 people paid by David to worship God! David's son, Solomon, continued the worship his dad had started in the Tabernacle of God. David was passionate about starting and continuing worship because God had directed Him to build a house of prayer:

(1 Chronicles 28:13) The king also gave Solomon the instructions concerning the work of the various divisions of priests and Levites in the Temple of the LORD. And he gave specifications for the items in the Temple that were to be used for worship.

(1 Chronicles 28:19) "Every part of this plan," David told Solomon, "was given to me in writing from the hand of the LORD."

Israel's great leaders, including Hezekiah, Josiah, Jehoshaphat, Zerubbabel, Ezra, and Nehemiah also followed David's example. The prophet Amos prophesied that in the last days the house of prayer established by David will be restored:

(Amos 9:11) "In that day I will restore the fallen house of David. I will repair its damaged walls. From the ruins I will rebuild it and restore its former glory.

This is what God is whispering to the hearts of many of His people in the Church right now. This is the call on my heart: to see night and day prayer established in my city. Is it on yours? Is there night and day prayer in your city already? How can you strengthen it? What talents and gifts has God placed in you for a time such as this? If there isn't night and day prayer in your city, how can you help to create it? God has the answers. He feels more passionate about establishing night and day prayer and worship in your city than even you do. Ask him how you can be a part of this important end-time plan. This is the time we are in! The time when God's end-time worship movement is beginning to take shape.

What We Believe Matters

Many people want to believe that Jesus will come and rapture His Church off of the planet before the Great Tribulation. Many people who truly love and serve Jesus hold this "pre-tribulation rapture" view and can find verses to support it. But consider who God is and what Jesus' objective is in releasing the judgments. He desires to save people. Saving people from hell, torment, and death is the reason He became a man and paid the price for sin. Would He do all that only to leave a confused and deceived group of humans on earth to blindly endure the wrath of the Great Tribulation, or would He establish His Church, His very body, in unity, power, and worship as a faithful witness of who He is and what He is doing? We should all search the Bible, and ask God to reveal to us His intentions for this time.

What we believe about the end-time worship movement, the building of the House of Prayer, and the unfolding of Jesus' battle plan, is extremely important. If we are just waiting to be removed from the earth by "surprise" one day before it gets "really bad," will we work hard to build the House of Prayer in our city in a meaningful way? We need God's help to figure out what time we live in, and what it means for us.

The rise of the end-time worship movements is really happening right now! The lines are being drawn and the sides are being taken. The social justice movement, a precursor to the Mystery Babylon religion, has made huge strides in the last 10 years. Many good-intentioned people are caught up in its seemingly noble mission. In almost every place where "social justice" is promoted, an intolerance of Israel and Jesus also appears. Social justice is incompatible with the justice Jesus will really deliver. There is no truth or justice apart from Jesus. Look at the end-time warnings Paul gave us in light of the Mystery Babylon:

(2 Thessalonians 2:3-11) …. For that day will not come until there is a great rebellion against God and the man of lawlessness (this is the antichrist) is revealed—the one who brings destruction. He will exalt himself and defy everything that people call god and every object of worship. He will even sit in the temple of God, claiming that he himself is God. Don't you remember that I told you about all this when I was with you?

And you know what is holding him back, for he can be revealed only when his time comes. For this lawlessness is already at work secretly, and it will remain secret until the one who is holding it back steps out of the way. Then the man of lawlessness will be revealed, but the Lord Jesus will kill him with the breath of His mouth and destroy him by the splendor of His coming. This man will come to do the work of Satan with counterfeit power and signs and miracles. He will use every kind of evil deception to fool those on their way to destruction, because they refuse to love and accept the truth that would save them. So God will cause them to be greatly deceived, and they will believe these lies.

(2 Corinthians 11:2-4) For I am jealous for you with the jealousy of God Himself. I promised you as a pure bride to one husband—Christ. But I fear that somehow your pure and undivided devotion to Christ will be corrupted, just as Eve was deceived by the cunning ways of the serpent. You happily put up with whatever anyone tells you, even if they preach a different Jesus than the One we preach, or a different kind of Spirit than the One you received, or a different kind of gospel than the one you believed.

Paul said that many people will be deceived because they refuse to love and accept the truth that would save them. The truth Paul was talking about was Jesus. Because the Mystery Babylon religion will claim to offer justice and peace, specifically "world peace", many good-intentioned people will want to align themselves with it. We need to love Jesus. He is "the Way, the Truth, and the Life." Any social justice or peace movement apart from Him is not real. In fact, it is evil.

The sad truth is, the Mystery Babylon and its followers will think they have won a great victory when the antichrist, one of their biggest supporters, achieves world peace. However, this is exactly when the antichrist will take off his peaceful mask and reveal exactly who He is, the man of lawlessness. He will destroy the Mystery Babylon religion and will kill any of its followers who don't agree to worship him (Revelation 17:16). This will be a dark day for those who have abandoned the truth for a lie. They will find themselves enslaved by the antichrist, who hates all religion and love.

United Worship Is Jesus' Plan

But the Church will be united in prayer. We will be a witness to God's love and glory. We will stand firm as a witness to Jesus, the Messiah. We will proclaim that the Lamb Who Was Slain is the only shelter in this time of great trouble. Through our worship and prayers, offered day and night, we will begin releasing, in partnership with Jesus, the judgments designed to drive evil off the planet. It is the end-time worship and prayer movement that will fill the bowls of God's wrath with prayer and incense. Look at what the Bible says our prayers will do:

> *(Revelation 8:3-5) Then another angel with a gold incense burner came and stood at the altar. And a great amount of incense was given to him to mix with the prayers of God's people as an offering on the gold altar before the throne. The smoke of the incense, mixed with the prayers of God's holy people, ascended up to God from the altar where the angel had poured them out. Then the angel filled the incense burner with fire from the altar and threw it down upon the earth; and thunder crashed, lightning flashed, and there was a terrible earthquake.*

You may be tempted to think all this trouble we are now seeing will pass. Information floods us from every direction. We get overloaded with other people's thoughts and interpretations about what is happening. My prayer is not that you would believe what I am saying about the time we live in. My prayer is that you would talk to God, search His Word, and decide for yourself what you believe. Living with a locked gaze on God is the only safe way to live, no matter what is going on around us. I'll end this chapter with the end-time warning given to the prophet Jeremiah:

(Jeremiah 23:16-22) This is what the LORD of Heaven's Armies says to His people: "Do not listen to these prophets when they prophesy to you, filling you with futile hopes. They are making up everything they say. They do not speak for the LORD! They keep saying to those who despise My word, 'Don't worry! The LORD says you will have peace!' And to those who stubbornly follow their own desires, they say, 'No harm will come your way!'

"Have any of these prophets been in the LORD's presence to hear what He is really saying? Has even one of them cared enough to listen? Look! The LORD's anger bursts out like a storm, a whirlwind that swirls down on the heads of the wicked. The anger of the LORD will not diminish until it has finished all He has planned. In the days to come you will understand all this very clearly. "I have not sent these prophets, yet they run around claiming to speak for Me. I have given them no message, yet they go on prophesying. If they had stood before Me and listened to Me, they would

have spoken My words, and they would have turned My people from their evil ways and deeds.

Where Do We Go From Here? - 8

You are part of a blessed generation that through the centuries God's people have longed to be a part of. How you see this time you live in (and the joy or fear you have in it) really is up to you. Jesus is proclaiming through His Word and His servants that He is the safe place in times of trouble. He is declaring that the bride (you) does not need to fear the plans of her loving husband (Jesus). Rumors about the end of the world, the unfolding of Jesus' amazing battle plan to drive evil off the planet, and the raising up of the end time worship movements will bring excitement and confusion to the world in ways it has never seen.

What does this all mean for you?! This is a question that runs through my mind daily. Finding out the answer...living out the answer...is one of my greatest desires. I want to see the greatness God has planned for me become real. To find out God's plans for me, and then to make choices that line my life up with what God says to do, is my definition of success. My prayer is that you will see success in your life this way. God desires greatness for you, too.

God has plans for you. He has put a desire for importance and greatness in your heart. He wants you to desire to be an important part of His plans for the earth. Whether you realize it or not, you *are* important. Connecting with God's heart and His plans for you will lead you to the future you would hope for (Jeremiah 29:11). Many people think desiring greatness in life is a sin. To some people it seems like the same thing as pride. God has placed a desire for greatness in everyone! What we do with our desire for greatness can lead to obedience or it can lead to pride and other sins. If you try to satisfy your desire for greatness the way the world says is good, by striving for worldly wealth, power, or fame, you will be disappointed. If you will take your God-given desire for greatness and connect it to God's plans for you, you will be amazed with what He will do through you. You were born for such a time as this.

What Can We Do Right Now?

In addition to God's specific plans for you, there are some general things I believe we are all called to do right now, as Jesus' plan to transition the age from darkness to the age of light begins to get more and more intense. I believe the most relevant instruction for our current time is found in Joel 2:12-13:

> *(Joel 2:12-13) That is why the LORD says, "Turn to Me now, while there is time. Give Me your hearts. Come with fasting, weeping, and mourning. Don't tear your clothing in your grief, but tear your hearts instead." Return to the LORD your God, for He is merciful and compassionate, slow to get angry and filled with unfailing love. He is eager to relent and not punish.*

We need to repent on behalf of the people we live with. Repenting just means to stop agreeing with the world's point of view, and agree with God wholeheartedly. It is tempting to think the people furthest from God should do the most repenting. That is not the way it works. God counts on those he calls "faithful" to lead repentance for those who can't see how dark their lives are. Think of the story of Daniel. He fasted and prayed for his people, even though he was one of the most righteous people in the land (Daniel 9:3). It was Abraham, the Father of Israel, who showed the most concern for Sodom.   The prophets, whose main concern was to know God and proclaim His messages, led the way in repentance for those who had no interest in knowing what was on God's heart.   Interceding in prayer, and turning wholeheartedly to God, as outlined in the Sermon on the Mount (Matthew 5, 6, and 7), is the key to changing the culture around us.

The whole point of Jesus' plan is to save the most people with the least severe means possible.   God takes no pleasure in pouring out His wrath; He takes pleasure in His people returning to Him in wholeheartedness.   God is the only safe place in a time of trouble.   Our main priority in these dark times should be what Jesus said was the most important commandment: Love the Lord your God with all your heart, mind, soul, and strength.   We love Him like this by pressing into Him for more of the Kingdom, remaining humble, showing mercy, loving those who oppose us, forgiving our enemies, giving secretly, fasting secretly, and resisting judgment of others, especially those who think we are wrong. This is the road to true happiness and a fiery heart for God.

We need to continually discern the time and what the Bible says about it. If we want to stay steady in loving God with our whole hearts, we need to trust Jesus' instructions in the Bible.   A few very important ones are set in my mind: setting our eyes on the things above (thinking about heaven), studying Jesus' end time plans (reading the book of Revelation and the other chapters in the Bible about Jesus' return), and watching for the unfolding of His plans to be able to explain to others why the world is experiencing trouble. We want to tell the world about Jesus' desire to partner with people, not crush them.   We need to be the messengers Jeremiah prophesied would tell people about Jesus' heart for them as His bride. Look at what the Bible says about Jesus' concern for the Bride:

> *(Ephesians 5:25-27) For husbands, this means love your wives, just as Christ loved the Church. He gave up His life for her to make her holy and clean, washed by the cleansing of God's word. He did this to present her to Himself as a glorious Church without a spot or wrinkle or any other blemish. Instead, she will be holy and without fault.*

Jesus plan is for us to prepare the Bride, Jesus' Church. We are Jesus' body on earth. It is our job, at Jesus' direction, to "wash and cleanse" the bride. I want to do everything in my power to make the Church spotless and wrinkle-free. That means I have decided in my heart to spend my time pressing into Jesus so that I can tell the Bride the truth about the time we live in, and how God feels about her. I must do this out of an overflow of what God is putting in my heart. You can only feed people with what you have. If you set your heart to press into God with all of your strength, you can't help but overflow into other lives.

Ask God for more hunger and thirst, more wisdom and revelation, more insight into His plans, more desire for His words, and more fascination with Jesus. He longs to give more and more of these things to you, but He is waiting on you to ask for them. God won't force you into this. If you will decide to press into God for more of His kingdom, you will overflow in a powerful way, and He will use you to lead many into His light. It might not seem like you are impacting many people, but in groups as small as one or two people God will change the world through you! If we are faithful with a little, He will give us much more now, *and* in the age to come (Luke 19:17).

We need to set our hearts to give our resources to God. I have decided in my heart to spend my money in a way that strengthens Jesus' bride to be wholehearted for Jesus. I might not always be faithful to do this well, but it is what I really want to do. You might not have a lot of money right now, but how you spend it and how you think about it REALLY matters. God owns everything. He isn't worried about having enough money! He wants you to see Him as your source and your reward in life. If you see Him as the owner of what you have and the one who provides everything you have, it will shape the way you see everything else. Money and time have a funny way of revealing what we REALLY believe. Decide to give it all to God, and He will show you how. This is the best deal ever, because He will make sure you have more than enough if you trust Him with all that you have. I have seen this happen in my life time, and time, and time again. God is faithful and wants you to test Him in this (Malachi 3:10)!

We need to intercede for Israel. Israel is God's special possession. They are the people He has decided to attach His name and promises to. We are blessed through Israel. We must know this. Time and time again, the world has come against Israel, and it is prophesied to happen again. We can already see it if we watch the news. Israel is surrounded by enemies. God promises a blessing to those who bless Israel, and a curse to those who don't (Genesis 12:3). Where we live is impacted by how the people in our area feel about Israel. If we, and the people we live near, spend our time interceding (praying like we care) for Israel, our land will be more blessed. Only when Jewish people in Jerusalem invite Jesus back as

Messiah, does He promise to return. This should be the cry of our hearts daily!

We need to get involved in the House of Prayer in our town. God is raising up a worship movement of night and day prayer all over the world. It is in the place of prayer the real power to change the world is found. God doesn't need us to formulate the plans and find the strength and resources to carry them out in our city. He has the plans, He has the resources. He wants the one thing we can give Him, our hearts. Night and day prayer is going to be the deciding factor in how blessed our cities are. If we cry out to Him day and night, God is faithful to protect and bless us (Luke 18:7). We want to be people after God's own heart, like David. David spent a huge amount of time and money establishing night and day prayer in Jerusalem, even going as far as to hire 4,000 musicians and singers to worship and pray (1 Chronicles 23:5).

God has given you unique talents that are needed for this time. Do you feel moved by someone else's need for prayer? That is the gift of intercession and The House of Prayer needs you! Do you have an ability to sing or play and instrument? The House of Prayer needs you! Do you have a gift of organization, encouragement, speaking, teaching, love kids, writing...the sky is the limit! The House of Prayer needs you! Begin the conversation with God to find out how He wants to use you.

The prophets told us night and day prayer was crucial to Jesus' plans to drive evil off the planet. It is believers, connected in unity in the House of Prayer, who will partner with God to release His power in the earth. Our prayers are the incense that fills the bowls in the book of Revelation (Revelation 5:8). Now is the time to connect with the House of Prayer and help build it in your city. If you don't have night and day prayer already in your city, ask God what your role is in establishing it. It will look differently in every city. God knows how to reach your city. God knows the beautiful music and emotions that will rise up before Him like incense from you and the other people in your town that connect with what He is doing. God knows the plans he has for your town. Press into His heart and ask Him to reveal His plans to you.

Resisting the "Normalcy Bias"

God's end time plans are intensifying all around us. If you watch for the conditions Jesus described as the "birth pangs," (Matthew 24) you will see them happening with greater and greater intensity and frequency. Darkness will increase, but so will light. Many people think that God is going to carry out His plans either way; that things will just work out. Things will work out, but how will they work out for you and the people you love? This is the real question.

In times of impending disaster, people often convince themselves that the situation will not really get that bad, so they do nothing to prepare for what is ahead. During World War II, Adolph Hitler, the leader of Germany, tried to exterminate Jewish people. Sadly, he was incredibly successful in his evil plan. Jewish people from many cities in Europe were put on trains and taken to concentration camps to die. For months, Jewish people were allowed to leave their homes and flee to a safe place. Many Jewish people who could have left did not leave.

Even as friends and neighbors were being carried away to their death, people with the resources to flee the trouble did not. They could not believe the worst would happen. Nothing like the holocaust had ever happened to them before, and they couldn't see the reality of it even as it unfolded right before their eyes. This phenomenon has been termed the "normalcy bias" by psychologists. If you have never experienced the Great Tribulation, it is easy to think it won't happen, even as it unfolds all around you. Our protection against the normalcy bias is reading the truth about God's plan in the Bible and talking to God about His plans.

In order to avoid thinking too much about the end of the age, many people use the excuse that Jesus said no one knows the day or the hour that He will return. That is true, but days and hours are very specific time-frames. Jesus himself said over and over that His followers should be watching and ready for His return. He said the generation that He returns to should recognize the signs. When the signs all happen in the same generation, that generation should know that it will not miss His coming. Look at what Jesus said:

> *(Luke 21:29-36) Then He gave them this illustration: "Notice the fig tree, or any other tree. When the leaves come out, you know without being told that summer is near. In the same way, when you see all these things taking place, you can know that the Kingdom of God is near.*
>
> *I tell you the truth, this generation will not pass from the scene until all these things have taken place. Heaven and earth will disappear, but My words will never disappear. "Watch out! Don't let your hearts be dulled by carousing and drunkenness, and by the worries of this life. Don't let that day catch you unaware, like a trap. For that day will come upon everyone living on the earth. Keep alert at all times. And pray that you might be strong enough to escape*

these coming horrors and stand before the Son of Man."

Look at people around you.   Will they be caught unaware?   Are the worries of this life crowding out an alertness about the days we live in? I believe you and I are that generation Jesus was talking about. I am not asking you to look down on, or judge, those around you. I am asking you to consider what this means for YOU. This isn't about what other people are doing or seeing, this is about what you are doing and seeing. You might be the one person in your sphere of influence who sees the days we are living in. No matter how old you are, you have REAL influence. You have access to the Holy Spirit and the most powerful throne in all of creation. YOU could change a city, or a state, or the world.

We Have to Know and Teach Revelation

Many people know a little about what the Bible says about the end of the age, and they love Jesus, but they just can't accept that what is happening around them is really the unfolding of Jesus' plans to drive evil off the planet. Because they can't discern the time, they miss the opportunity to prepare and partner with Jesus in a meaningful way. They haven't really studied Revelation or the other parts of the Bible that talk about Jesus' return, but instead rely on the vague things they learned in Sunday school or from chatting with other believers.

The Book of Revelation is one of the only books in the Bible with a promise of blessing to those who read it, yet it is one of the least taught books in Church. Look at what Revelation says:

(Revelation 1:3) God blesses the one who reads the words of this prophecy to the Church, and He blesses all who listen to its message and obey what it says, for the time is near.

No matter what anyone else believes about Revelation, you would be wise to take the Bible's advice to heart! Jesus has so many plans for us, but He won't force us into them. It is up to us to decide to discern the time we live in, find out what the Bible says about it, and then press into God for direction. My prayer for you is that you will start to talk to God about the words and ideas in this book. Don't take my word for anything! Reading someone's thoughts about what the Bible says may give you more information, but it will rarely move your heart. Talking to God about what He thinks will move your heart in powerful ways. Begin the conversation with the Lord. He is able to show you the truth. He is the only safe place, no matter what is happening in the earth.

Made in the USA
Charleston, SC
29 November 2013